THE HABIT OF CRITICAL THINKING

*Change Your Mind and Sharpen Your Thoughts
With These Powerful Routines
(2022 Guide for Beginners)*

Daphne Elliott

CONTENTS

INTRODUCTION

"All truths are easy to understand once they are discovered; the point is to discover them" - Galileo Galilei

How often do you feel compelled to choose between professional and personal success? That life is an unwinnable compromise in which you feel you fall short despite your best efforts?

You want to do a good job, to get things right the first time, and to work efficiently in terms of time and money. You could be in charge of setting a good example for others, keeping them motivated, and delivering good results without dropping the ball or causing too much stress. You don't want to be pushy or greedy; you just want to be your best. You've most likely worked hard and carefully considered your options along the way.

The catch is that being who you need to be at work often means sacrificing who you want to be at home. Missed opportunities may haunt you at times, and the prospect of escaping the rat race may taunt you on bad days. Some people appear to have it all because of luck or inheritance, but where is the just reward for decent hard work?

You can regain that balance by using your brain. You already have the skills, but they must be recognized and practiced, just like any other skill. You can be successful at work without constantly sacrificing your personal and social life for your job. It's also a lot easier than you think, and it's completely free. All you have to do is identify old auto-pilot behaviors that are no longer useful to you and replace them with smarter, upgraded ones.

Consider it a software update for your phone or computer. It makes things go more smoothly. If you continued to use the original operating system, your device would be extremely slow. It does not necessitate the purchase of a new phone. You simply need to recognize that an update is required and then set aside a short amount of time for that update to occur, resulting in significant time savings down the road.

This book will guide you through the process of updating your brain. By developing these critical thinking habits, you will improve your approach to challenges, make more reasonable professional and personal decisions, and improve your outlook on solving future problems more effectively and independently.

So, what do I know about education? Why did I write this book? I am a scientist and a teacher, and I still enjoy the challenge of learning new things. I've seen what works and what doesn't, and I've had plenty of chances to make mistakes and try again. If you've ever heard the expression "ask a busy person if you need something is done," that has been my life. I've been that 'busy person' who is always adding to their to-do list. It hasn't yet sunk me.

After turning 30, I was promoted to lead a large secondary school science team in a new school, co-ordinated the relocation of lab equipment and teaching materials to a new building within the first term of employment, moved house myself, got married, and ran my first marathon. I consider that seven-month spell success because I am still in my job, house, and marriage, and I have a few more marathons under my belt. It was insane, but it taught me how to use the skills I already had more effectively and provided me with the opportunity to learn many new ones. I had more fun and accomplished more than I ever imagined possible in such a short period of time.

My academic background and love of learning led me to become a teacher, and I continue to stay up to date on the latest research and success stories about how people learn best. Teaching and education are much more to me than a way to get a grade on a piece of paper. Education is about learning to use your mind effectively and discovering new things.

To be successful in life, you must constantly learn new facts, skills, and methods. You must be able to think critically in order to learn effectively. I enjoy the sciences because they provide a direct way to investigate the physical world around us, but every subject necessitates an investigative approach in order to dig deeper and discover more.

This is the subject of this book. Identifying the skills you most likely already have makes them more explicit and transforms them into habits that will serve you well for many years to come.

Are you ready to update your mind and reboot your autopilot thinking? Continue reading.

Claire Johnson

1
HOW TO THINK LIKE A THINKER

Your Holidays Are Really Experiments

"The scientific method is just the normal working of the human mind" – Thomas Henry Huxley.

Do you believe that the science experiments you performed in school were solely for the purpose of earning a good grade, drawing neat diagrams of strange equipment, and plotting graphs? Consider again! You can apply what you learned in class to discover new options and opportunities. All you need to do is revise a little.

My role as a science teacher is to teach students scientific facts and to help them solve problems using the scientific method.

To be a good scientist, you must have critical thinking as your default mode. This, however, does not imply acting like a Vulcan!

You can be completely logical in your approach to life while also being emotionally aware. Being a true critical thinker necessitates empathy.

Critical thinking does not imply preferring to follow your head over your heart. It is necessary to consider both in order to reach the best conclusion. Scientists are stereotyped as having the emotional range of a teaspoon, but this is only a stereotype. Stereotypes are the polar opposite of critical thinking.

So, what exactly is our scientific methodology? In short, a scientist will first notice something unusual, such as a penicillin mold that prevents bacteria from growing around it. They will then pose an investigational question, such as 'can I repeat this to stop different types of bacteria growing near the mold?' or 'will using more mold kill more bacteria?' They will devise a strategy to test this by conducting experiments and collecting data, which they will use to reach a conclusion and answer their original question. In reality, it is common in science, as it is in life, to find the answer to one question, which opens the door to many others and allows you to seek more answers.

This method is not limited to science. You've most likely used it without even thinking about it.

Observing and Inquiring

Let us plan your next vacation. Whether you've been saving for it or not, the main goal when you start planning is to get it right.

You most likely begin by 'observing' what you and your family require. Is everyone tired and in need of a break? Is it necessary for them to embark on a grand adventure and see something new? Have you all had enough of your weather and want to go somewhere else? Essentially, why do you require that vacation? What need are you attempting to meet?

Establishing the goals of your vacation requires you to honestly question yourself, but it also requires you to seek the opinions of whoever you are traveling with. If you want to have a successful vacation, you may need to compromise on your goals. Going into the process having already decided where you want to go and then persuading others that you are correct is unlikely to meet everyone's needs.

When you've decided on a vacation destination and goals, you can ask friends or Google for recommendations. You can inquire about price, weather, transportation, lodging, entertainment, and other topics. It is best to approach both critical thinking and vacation planning with an open mind.

Concluding And Testing

Choosing your destination is analogous to deciding which experiment to conduct.

You don't know if it will meet your requirements; you're testing and gathering data by taking a vacation. The holiday is the subject of your investigation! Is it going to fulfill its original purpose?

You can form your conclusion at the end of the vacation. Are you feeling more relaxed, energized, or tanned? We all do it automatically; we decide if it was a 'good' vacation and if we would go there again. We either recommend it to our friends or advise them to avoid it.

Sometimes holiday 'experiments' deliver exactly what we hoped for. They don't always! My parents decided to take us to Spain for a vacation when I was about twelve years old. We'd been there before in October, and there was a lot to see and do, as well as beautiful beaches! It appeared to be a sound strategy. The 'experiment,' the holiday itself, demonstrated that there was a flaw in this plan. Summers in Spain are extremely hot. We're English, and we're not very good at being that hot. We needed a siesta in the afternoons, and the only time we could handle exploring the area was late in the evenings and into the night. I recall being at a funfair at 1 a.m. My parents claimed that they slept less on vacation than if we had stayed at home, and we concluded that Spain was not the best option for a summer vacation for our family.

I still use this information to plan vacations. I discovered that I dislike being in hot places. Developing a thorough understanding of oneself aids the critical thinking process. It's like knowing a few more rules to help you make better decisions in the future.

You can think critically if you can plan a vacation. All of the skills are already present. All you have to do is set them as your new autopilot.

Why Is 'Being Right' the Wrong Way to Go?
When was the last time you went for a hike? If it was a popular route, there would have been numerous paths leading to the summit.

Nonetheless, the question is: have you done any research before embarking on this journey? Do you consider your abilities and the resources you have to achieve your goals before taking any action? For example, before going on a hike, take a good look at the available paths, where they lead, and what kind of equipment you'll need. This can mean the difference between a wonderful and a painful experience.

You don't want to take a path that requires you to do some rock climbing to reach the summit if you only have hiking boots and don't know how to use a rope. You don't want to choose a path simply because it begins at the nearest car park or appears to be the shortest on the map, without gathering more evidence and considering alternative routes. That short path may be the most treacherous and dangerous. Choosing a path based on a hunch can be dangerous!

Our default mode of thought is frequently like taking that short but unresearched path. We'll go with the option that appears to be the simplest at first glance. If we don't think about it anymore, don't ask any questions, and don't look for evidence, we'll end up on a potentially dangerous path at random.

To think critically, we must switch our autopilot to one that follows the scientific method. Consider the objectives, questions, plan, experiment, and conclusion that are required. To accomplish this effectively, we must begin with an open mind. You don't plan an experiment by deciding what the outcome will be ahead of time. Experiments are all about discovering answers and being ready to be surprised!

The first key to critical thinking is to not decide on a conclusion before you begin thinking. You must think before you form your arguments and make your decisions, rather than looking for evidence to support what you have already decided is your truth.

It may appear obvious when written down, but this is the most significant barrier that most people face. This is due to the fact that most of us prefer to be correct. We like to appear intelligent. Thinking and making decisions with an open mind implies that there is a real possibility that the way we have been operating up to this point is not the best way to proceed. Perhaps someone else has a better suggestion. Perhaps we've been on the wrong track because we made a default decision and discovered halfway through that it wasn't the best option. Is it better to keep going despite the fact that the road ahead is uncertain and potentially dangerous? Or should you take the time to go back and try again?

The latter implies that we must accept that we did not make the best decision. It could even mean that as we make a new plan, a friend will say, 'I told you so!' It entails being humble enough to honestly consider the opinions of others. Thinking critically entails engaging in this type of slow thinking,' which prevents us from jumping to conclusions and then being too proud to back down.

Critical thinkers seek the truth. They gather the evidence before drawing conclusions. They are open to new ideas and admitting mistakes without taking them personally. It should not be considered shameful to admit that someone else had a better idea, but our modern society frequently makes us feel as if we have failed. However, simply believing something is correct does not make it the best choice. As it is said, the truth will set you free, so embrace it even if it did not come from you.

Improve Your Skills to Shake Up Your Thinking
It is in our nature to think, but it is not in our nature to think well. We have easily led astray and distracted.

Being a truth-seeker entails re-calibrating your thinking. To improve the traits that make a critical thinker, you need the right mindset, certain character traits, awareness of predispositions and limitations, and a lot of practice. This isn't as difficult as it sounds; we're all born with these abilities. We simply live in a fast-paced world where we take shortcuts that become habits and stop thinking clearly.

We can create a new and improved auto-pilot with a few changes.

Learning is not the same as thinking, and knowledge is not the same as understanding. I can get a student to recite a definition in order to get a good grade on a test, but that only tests their memory, not their scientific understanding. In our modern world, where most facts can be found in a matter of seconds, we are still led to believe that someone who knows a lot of points has a true understanding of a subject.

Knowledge is important; solid basic knowledge serves as a foundation for understanding. The ability to read and write a language does not automatically qualify you as a poet. However, you cannot be a poet unless you first have that knowledge.

Our minds can't hold a lot of information in our short-term memories and use it to solve complex problems. How well we can solve problems is determined by our cognitive load. If you want to improve your ability to solve problems in a specific area, you must first ensure that you have the necessary knowledge.

To develop the ability to be a critical thinker, you must first develop your scientific skill set, much like a scientist who has completed their research and is ready to begin their experiment. If you master these, critical thinking will become your default pattern in your long-term memory for all of your decision-making. Prior to that point, you must practice, just as you would when learning a new phone number or a routine.

Identification, analysis, interpretation, interference, evaluation, explanation, and self-reflection will be part of your skillset. You may already use these on a daily basis, either in your job or in your thinking. The key is to apply them consistently in both your personal and professional life.

Identification Is Critical

Identification may appear simple, but it is frequently the most difficult skill to master.

Consider a problem you'd like to solve. Most of us have big ideas. Then we either panic about the enormity of the task ahead and do nothing, or we create a massive to-do list and become increasingly anxious as we struggle to make progress. This is why the majority of New Year's resolutions fail.

The most common New Year's resolutions are to get healthier, which is often broken down into 'do more exercise' and 'lose some weight.' These may appear to be good goals, but they are not! In these resolutions, there is no identification of the actual root problem or achievable solutions. They are overly broad. Most people give up when they first want to eat cake or when they don't feel like going for a run.

Consider the path up the mountain once more. The most important thing was to get started in the right direction. Everything else is dependent on that small decision to identify the best starting point, the best place to park and begin.

If you want to lose weight, the best way to start is to identify one small aspect of your life that will help. Maybe you realize you need to eat breakfast at home instead of grabbing a less healthy snack with a coffee before work. Perhaps you've realized that you need to switch from sugary drinks to versions with less sugar. Perhaps, like me, you've decided that the best way to avoid being tempted by chocolate is to simply stop buying it?! A small, manageable change can have a large impact. That alone indicates that you are more likely to succeed and then identify your next issue.

Your pivot point is identification. If you clearly define your problem, you will be able to find the right solution. From there, things get a lot easier. However, start small and specific.

The next skill you'll learn is analysis.

Examine That

This is where your Vulcan logic comes into play. It is about approaching the data or the language with no preconceptions, emotion, bias, or excuses. Consider the scientists who must record all trends or patterns in their findings, including those they did not anticipate. Or, how the lawyers are required to analyze the information provided to them and summarise their findings, even if it means admitting something their client did that they would have preferred remained unknown.

If you want to lose weight, you should do the same thing - you should examine your diet. You must be truthful about what you eat, how much you eat, and when you eat it. You should keep track of whether you eat more when you are out, stressed, or with friends. All of this is viewed as cold, hard data by critical thinkers. Even if we don't like what we see, analysis entails seeing the big picture and patterns.

As a result, many people believe they are adept at analyzing their lives but are not. They only examine the information that they allow themselves to see. As a scientist, you can only analyze data after the entire experiment has been completed. To create a good graph, you must have all of your data.

Interpretation Is Possible

After you've examined what's going on, you can begin to draw conclusions. This is commonly referred to as inference. Remember that it comes after data collection, not before!

When was the last time you went over your finances? Did you keep track of what you spent, when you spent it, and where you spent it?

Perhaps your data indicated that you spend a lot of time on eBay at night. Or perhaps all of those little cups of take-out coffee add up to a significant portion of your food bill. If that's the case, you might conclude that you're more likely to overspend when you're tired (late at night, early in the morning) and not paying attention to your spending. Spending is a result of your mental state.

Conclusions frequently require you to select your future self. It could mean deciding to try something new or breaking a bad habit.

This is why it is critical to stick to the method; a wrong conclusion may lead to incorrect future actions.

Life, on the other hand, is rarely as simple as providing black and white answers. You and a friend can look at the same data and reach different conclusions. It doesn't necessarily imply that either of you is incorrect or correct! To think critically, you must be open to the possibility of alternate interpretations.

For example, my husband frequently looks out the window and declares, "It's pouring outside; I'll go for a run later." I can look outside and classify the same weather as merely 'drizzle,' which is no reason to avoid going for a run. We can look at the same evidence and reach completely different conclusions. Neither of us can claim that our 'truth' is the only one that exists. We simply reach different conclusions.

Bias In Evaluation

As a critical thinker, whenever you reach a conclusion, especially one that necessitates a change in your behavior, you must ask yourself, "Is what I've discovered the truth?" You must ensure that it is as accurate and free of bias as possible. This is an assessment.

This skill requires you to frequently play the role of the devil's advocate. Do you believe the data? Is it possible that the data will lead to a different conclusion? Is there anything missing or something you know but haven't revealed?

Consider the previous example of spending. Do you pay for some coffees with cash so that they don't appear on your credit card bill? Or are you the person in charge of the office coffee machine, and many of those coffees were not for you?

Anyone can analyze data and draw conclusions. Strangers could draw conclusions based on your bank statements. Some of them may be correct. Others might not. Because you are the only one who has the complete picture, you are the only one who can evaluate these conclusions.

Following the evaluation, you have the option of accepting or rejecting the conclusion. If you reject it because the conclusion was flawed, you would typically go back to the beginning and gather a more complete set of data to reach a more accurate conclusion the next time.

Explanation

When you follow the steps outlined above, you will occasionally arrive at conclusions that do not appear obvious.

I wanted to improve my marathon times while training. I reasoned that if I ran more frequently and for longer distances, this would suffice. It was effective, but only up to a point. I was unable to run a half marathon in under two hours. I got it down to 2 hours, 10 seconds, and 4 seconds. But I never really progressed. It was exasperating! I looked at a wider range of training plans and focused on including hill sprints and 5k park runs in my weekly routine. It worked, but it only saved me about 5 minutes. My conclusions influenced my actions, but not the outcomes.

I then realized that I had only been concentrating on analyzing data from my runs. It appears logical, but it led me to a blind spot—my diet. I've always been healthy, so I didn't think of my diet as potential data. I didn't think it would have an impact on my time, but I was mistaken.

Convinced that there was something else going on, I sought medical advice and discovered that I have lactose intolerance. So I gave up dairy, and every race I ran after that was a new personal best. My husband often missed me at finish lines because I was often ten minutes ahead of schedule!

Others inquired as to what I had done to cause such a drastic change in my race times. I had to explain that I was doing nothing different; aside from that, I had stopped eating dairy products, which would not work for most people. It sparked debate, so I had to learn how to explain my conclusion to people who thought it sounded like a passing fad or a joke. They had hoped for a running tip, but they had not received it!

Exercising intensely for long periods of time stresses our bodies and makes the gut more sensitive. This means that even minor food allergies can cause problems during intense training or racing.

Another critical thinking skill is the ability to clearly explain your actions, particularly those that do not appear to be obvious decisions. It's similar to writing a book synopsis. Before the listener switches off, you must communicate your reasoning and conclusions. If you explain too briefly, you will only invite more questions. People will tune out if you explain for too long.

Self-Reflection

The final skill in the critical thinking toolkit has nothing to do with decision-making. This one is a little more personal.

Scientists study-specific sciences for a variety of reasons. It could be a particularly interesting topic; they might want to learn something new or broaden their career options. None of these very valid reasons influenced my decision to major in chemistry. I chose my A-level subjects and then my degree subjects based on what required the least amount of writing.

The irony that I am writing a book is not lost on me. I enjoy writing now, but in my early twenties, I preferred numbers to words every time. With the exception of the occasional dissertation, this worked well; labs were mostly math, and organic chemistry required a lot of drawing. Then I went through teacher training. We had to write a lot of essays, especially self-reflective ones. I felt like a rabbit caught in the headlights. I aspired to teach science to children. Why did I feel compelled to write these pieces?

I didn't realize it at the time, but the essays were helpful. Being aware of your intentions and motivations is what self-reflection entails. It is a skill that is rarely taught, certainly not in a chemistry degree, but it is frequently the difference between making progress and stagnating in any area of your life.

To be skilled at self-reflection, you must ask yourself one question repeatedly: 'why?'

What motivates you to want certain things? Why are you feeling the way you do?

Why do you want to achieve certain things? Why do you believe 'X' will make your life better?

To do so, you must know yourself as well as step outside of yourself. In your professional life, you may have completed a '360' analysis or determined your Myers-Briggs personality type. These are good starting points, but you must understand how they apply to your personal and professional lives.

Playing a real game like the Sims is a good way to practice self-reflection in your daily life. You're doing the self-reflection for the characters you're in charge of. You can do this well because you are familiar with the exact characteristic breakdowns and needs of those fictitious pixel beings. You can tell if they are extroverted and should socialize more, if they are tired and should relax more, or if they are playful and should play more. You can also see what they need to do to advance in their careers and relationships. You understand their needs and have the big picture to guide them to do what is best for them at any given time.

What if you could easily 'check' your own needs and motivations? How much easier would it be to do the next right thing? This level of introspection enables us to be more efficient in developing the best habits for our lives.

Characteristics of a Winner

Critical thinking skills are a toolkit that can be used to structure and guide decision-making. They are something you should do and practice.

The critical thinking characteristics are something you should strive for and practice. The skills will always feel forced if these characteristics are not developed.

The goal, according to critical thinking experts Richard Paul and Linda Elder, is to become an "accomplished thinker" by practicing the techniques and developing certain characteristics until critical thinking becomes your autopilot. Both are necessary.

Unfortunately, both ourselves and our society are major impediments to this.

However, once acknowledged, you can easily overcome these obstacles! As Matt Haig points out, you can't put out a fire by ignoring it.

So, what is the nature of your society? How can it influence the way you think? Consider what you would consider 'normal.' How does it appear? What would your 'normal job,' 'normal family,' and 'normal house' look like? The irony is that most of us want to be normal while also standing out from the crowd. We want to be just normal enough to feel like we belong while also being distinctive.

This is natural; we are social creatures, and society evolved by establishing expectations and rules for the group to follow in order for it to succeed.

Some rules remain (don't murder others), while others do not (always carry a bale of hay in your cart).

However, in order to be normal enough to be accepted, we frequently end up behaving like sheep without even realizing it.

Keep an open mind
A friend recently updated her Facebook location and marital status, about two and a half years after the events themselves. One person congratulated her, which is understandable given that many of us have social media acquaintances who are not up to date on our personal lives. Someone else then wished her a happy anniversary, knowing she was married and assuming the update was on the anniversary of this. She suddenly received a flood of messages wishing her a happy anniversary. Some of these were even submitted by guests who had attended the wedding!

We see other people's messages online and copy them because we don't want to be the one who forgets a significant date. We don't always check first, even when we should know better based on personal experience! The more people who say something is true, the less likely we are to disagree. We are more likely to doubt ourselves than we are to doubt popular opinion.

Conformity is not always a bad thing; however, if done unthinkingly, it can lead to bad habits and strongly held stereotypes.

Critical thinkers are in control of their thoughts and beliefs. They dare to do so even when it goes against what is considered "normal" in their society.

Many brilliant new ideas would not have gained traction if their creators had been timid. Consider the printing press, which was a huge step forward in spreading education to all people, regardless of class.

It was, however, strongly opposed, with Conrad Gessner writing to authorities to have it banned because he was concerned that it would result in a "confusing and harmful abundance of books." What is novel or unusual is frequently feared.

A healthy form of skepticism is having the courage to question the norm. It does not imply that you are a pessimist! It means you want to be certain that you are receiving accurate information. To do this well, simply ask yourself, "Am I sure this is true?" for each topic. It's really simple!

A word of caution: healthy skepticism may be misinterpreted by others as mistrust. It may imply requesting evidence rather than accepting a statement at face value, even from someone you trust. If you are not convinced, request to see the articles and generally ask awkward questions! A good question to ask yourself (and others) is, "Is this a fact or an opinion masquerading as a fact?"

Any social media platform is a good place to practice this. Do you believe that the posts you see represent the objective truth?

Keep an open mind

Curiosity and inquisitive thinking are a small step away from skepticism.

When you stop automatically accepting the information presented to you by society, you will be able to be more curious about your surroundings.

It gives you the mental freedom to think about 'what if...?' more frequently.

Galileo is a wonderful example of this. He (correctly) defied popular belief at the time by claiming that the Earth orbited the Sun rather than the other way around. While other astronomers developed increasingly complex models to explain the movements of the planets across the night sky, Galileo used his new 'telescope' to support his alternative theory. He stopped assuming that the current theory was correct, which allowed him to be inquisitive while others struggled to fit their data into an existing conclusion. Those in power at the time refused to look through his telescope or even consider the evidence. Galileo was not well-liked for his discovery, but he was correct.

Keep an open mind.

Open-mindedness is the polar opposite of lazy thinking and is frequently a victim of our society's expectations. Stereotypes are humanity's method of making faster decisions about who to trust. They are, however, the enemy of critical thinkers and the epitome of sloppy thinking. Stereotypes exist to keep us from thinking, which is why they are so dangerous.

To be open-minded, you must be aware of your own stereotypes. Everyone has them; they are a result of the society we grew up in. So think about it. Consider why you believe someone will behave in a certain way. If you find it difficult to do this on yourself, consider those closest to you, such as family and close contacts. It's likely that you share some of the same stereotypes.

Stereotypes are contagious. Make sure you know yours and then test them by asking questions and responding honestly.

Maintain Objectivity

After you've worked on removing your personal biases, you can use the critical thinking toolkit to examine the issues objectively. It entails seeing reality rather than a mirage. Even when shopping, objectivity is a beneficial state of mind to cultivate. What do you require, and what are impulse buys? Which items do you purchase based on what others expect of you? Remove the emotion from these small decisions to see how it affects your choices.

Keep an open mind

The other impediment to critical thinking is our sense of self.

Being able to master these characteristics means the difference between being a self-serving' critical thinker and a 'fair-minded' critical thinker. I'm sure you can tell which one you prefer just by looking at the titles!

The self-serving critical thinker is highly rational and can use critical thinking effectively, but only for their own benefit. They purposefully use arguments to confuse and manipulate others. You will be better than that because the flaw of self-serving critical thinkers is that their thinking is always biased. So it's not critical thinking at all, just a figment of one's imagination.

Be Grateful

There is so much to learn that it is difficult to consider what you have yet to learn and what you may never be able to learn. It is sometimes easier to pretend that we know everything there is to know about a subject.

This is where humility comes in handy. Humility entails not assuming you know best or that the best solution is the one that benefits you.

It is an odd truth that the more capable a person is at a task, the more likely they are to underrate and underestimate their ability. There is growing interest in 'imposter syndrome,' a condition in which "high-achieving individuals attribute their accomplishments to luck and contingency rather than individual skill and merit." This is not what being humble entails; you can acknowledge your strengths, but you must also be aware of your weaknesses. It's a delicate balancing act.

Be Forgiving

When you can accept different points of view and perspectives without taking them personally, you know you're getting close to mastering critical thinking skills. Finding out you're wrong while searching for the truth excites critical thinkers. It broadens one's horizons and opens up new possibilities.

Be adaptable

Finally, in a world where talking about flexibility usually means discussing a yoga class or admitting to 'giving in' to someone else's request, this useful trait is frequently undervalued. This summary is provided by a (fairly) well-known Lao Tzu quote.

"Men are born soft and supple; when they die, they become stiff and hard." Plants are born tender and pliant; when they die, they become brittle and dry. As a result, anyone who is stiff and inflexible is a disciple of death. "Whoever is soft and yielding is a life disciple."

Flexibility does not imply a lack of conviction in your beliefs. It means that when life changes, as it always does, you can realign rather than break.

And, regardless of what you believe, life will change. Sometimes by choice, but more often than not. You'll have to adjust. Beliefs and habits that have served you well in the past will need to be reviewed and updated. If you are willing to open your eyes and look, you may be surprised at the opportunities that may present themselves.

Steps to Take

You know what you should do, but how are you going to do it? Here is a list of brain games to get you started.

1. Purchase a puzzle book or app, focusing on logic crosses or sudoku.
   These rely on your ability to analyze and interpret data rather than knowledge or observation.
2. Disprove your stereotypes: when you walk down the street, ask yourself, "What do they do for a living?" 'Where do they reside?'

If you have biases, an answer will most likely come to mind; make a note of it so you know where you need to check yourself in the future.

3. Find an article that interests you online or in a newspaper, and then try to find the same story reported elsewhere. Are there any distinctions? Are you able to locate the primary source data? This will increase your awareness of what sources you can trust while also broadening your reading!

4. Consider what you wore today: ask yourself why you chose those items, and what image you want to project to others. It's a good place to start when trying to figure out what motivates you.

5. Choose a nearby item and consider how it came to be there. What material is it made of? What caused it to appear? Who was involved in its creation? Who created it? Why did they create it? This gets you in the habit of asking questions and considering different options.

6. Rather than writing it down, try to keep a running total of costs when shopping or scores when playing a game. Not only will it improve your memory, but it will also improve your numeracy, allowing you to analyze information faster and spot potential errors sooner.

7. Dissect complex problems and solutions as if you were explaining them to a 6-year-old. See how simple you can make it while maintaining meaning. You will improve your explanation skills if you can learn to be precise while remaining concise. 13

8. Try using the critical thinking process the next time you plan a trip or an evening in: identify your goals, ask questions to form a plan, and then analyze your options. This will aid you in the process while also providing numerous opportunities for self-reflection.

When you've decided to spend quality time with a friend, you're less likely to end up binge-watching TV. You will plan activities that will help you achieve your goals. You will choose a mountain path that is safe for you once you have acknowledged your experience.

Once you've identified your own biases, you'll be able to appreciate a broader range of viewpoints and make more balanced decisions.

Critical thinking skills will enable you to reclaim control of your time and your life path. You can begin to form the habits you want and abandon the ones that are holding you back.

That's a compelling reason to reconsider the scientific method.

Summary of the Chapter

- Consider yourself a scientist – your decisions are experiments.
- Observe, forecast, plan, execute, conclude, and evaluate.
- Consider what you do and work to improve your toolkit of skills, which includes identification, analysis, interpretation, evaluation, explanation, and self-reflection.
- Consider how you do it: make sure that society's expectations or your ego do not influence your decisions.
- Continue to return to a few key questions. What evidence do I have that this is correct? What is the reason for this? Is it equitable for all parties involved?

2
WHAT HABITS ARE ALL ABOUT

"We are what we repeatedly do. Excellence, then, is not an act, but a habit." — Aristotle

Have you ever stood by a fridge or a cupboard, mindlessly eating something while your mind raced through your to-do list for the day? You opened the door and got the food out, but it may feel like your autopilot is doing it and you never really chose it. It's so easy to get lost in our heads and thoughts that we sleepwalk through even the most basic decisions. But why is that? And how do we bring ourselves back to reality? To reclaim control of our lives, we must relinquish control of our questioning minds, which will keep us from eating the entire bag of popcorn, or much more.

Habits are actions and behaviors that we perform automatically, ranging from simple daily routines to physical and mental activities that we've learned over time. Because habits can be good or bad for us, we need to understand how they form and are forgotten so that we can use them positively in our lives.

Your habits define you

When our auto-pilot is not the one we want, we develop bad habits. One major reason we often follow our default behavior rather than pausing to consider a particular option is a stress.

You may already be aware that stress weakens the prefrontal cortex, the part of the brain responsible for working memory . This is why, despite the fact that choosing a pizza topping is generally a low-stakes decision, it can be difficult. You lose your ability to reason.

If these 'blips' in thought were limited to food, the only thing that might suffer is your waistline. However, we have the ability to go into autopilot or decision-free mode in all aspects of our lives, from jobs to relationships.

It's why people long for hindsight without realizing that, most of the time, the situation could have been handled better by stopping, getting off the default-decision travelator, and thinking clearly. The majority of people are afraid to ask themselves what they want and why they want it. This is frequently due to the fact that it may provide them with an uncomfortable answer or require them to take action, adding to their already impossible to-do list.

This is where the well-known fast versus slow thinking mode comes into play .

Our fast-mode involves default behaviors, which are automatic and quick responses to situations; these can be good or bad, but they are where our "bad habits" take root. We can also go into slow mode, which involves, you guessed it, slowing down to think through a situation logically. Herein lies the issue. We aren't very good at slowing down, so we aren't always very good at thinking clearly about what we're doing or why we're doing it.

So, the next time you find yourself unintentionally attached to your favorite snack bag, try slowing down. Try to figure out why you're eating it, what you should do instead, and how you can avoid ending up in the same place again. In my case, this entails concealing the popcorn on the top shelf.

Simply by beginning to ask the right questions, you can learn a lot more about who you are, what motivates you, and where you want to go in life. You can change your habits by starting with small decisions and working your way up to the big ones. Your habits shape your opportunities in the future.

Fortunately, changing habits does not require luck or perseverance. There are well-researched frameworks you can use to logically introduce new habits or eliminate bad ones. So, what do you wish to alter?

Unpicking Your Autopilot system
Consider something you do frequently. Maybe it's how you get ready in the morning or how you leave the house. You almost certainly

perform certain steps in a specific order. As you leave your house, you double-check that you have your phone and keys. When you've finished your drink, you put your mug in the dishwasher. After a workout, you wash your gym clothes. Or maybe you hit the snooze button on your alarm for a while before getting out of bed, and you get breakfast and coffee at the same place on your way to work. There will be plenty of 'in place' patterns that are easy to find if you look for them.

You can use a pattern to identify and understand new habits in any area of your life, whether physical or mental.

This pattern is known as the 'Habit Loop,' and it serves as a cue, a routine, and a reward. For example, you might get up early every morning (cue), eat breakfast (routine), and have an energized body (reward) ready to greet the day. As a result, you are aware that feeling energetic is associated with waking up and eating breakfast every morning.

If you receive a positive response, you are more likely to continue this habit.

We constantly use this habit loop on other people and even animals. Have you ever seen a dog being trained to sit? The dog hears the cue, sits (as is customary), and receives a treat (reward). Finally, the dog will sit on command even if it does not receive a treat because it may receive a treat at any time. Because the dog associates sitting with a reward, the command makes the dog want to sit. Intermittently obtained rewards can even more strongly enforce behavior than rewards that are always present 4. This is why gambling is addictive; you never know if your next bet will pay off. The uncertain but real promise of a possible victory motivates you to try again and again. Your reward must be something you desire, but it does not have to occur on a regular basis. So if you wake up early, eat breakfast, and prepare well for the day but still have a bad day, it doesn't mean you should abandon that habit. You are aware that this habit usually results in a better day, so you continue to practice it.

Habits, by definition, are not one-time events. This is where the name 'Habit Loop' comes from, as positive feedback drives the continuous cycle. Habits, whether good or bad, will keep repeating themselves like a broken record unless the loop is broken.

This is where your critical thinking abilities can come in handy.

Consider the steps in the habit loop. They can all be broken down into questions to assist you in identifying what is going on in your head and untangling your autopilot.

Cue - What motivates you to do it? Make observations about your own life. Keep an eye out for trends and patterns that precede your action. It could be a feeling, a time of day, another action, or even a specific smell that causes your reaction. This may take some time, but it is a great way to increase self-awareness. Consider it a fun challenge to figure out what these cues are.

What do you do on a daily basis? This is the simple part because it is usually a physical action that you perform. This is what you categorize as a 'good' or a 'bad' habit.

Reward - Why do you keep doing it? Habits repeat themselves for a reason.

What is the underlying cause of your identified habit? What is the incentive that drives you to do the same thing over and over? It could be a physical reward (such as a sugar or adrenaline rush) or an emotional reward (you feel relaxed or happy). This is the most effective part of the habit loop. You might not stick to the habit if you don't have a really good reward.

You can rework the habit into what you want it to be once you understand the habit loop.

The Golden Rule of Habit Exchange

When you're bored, you'll have a routine that you stick to.

Everybody does it. You can check your phone for social interaction if you want to. You might be able to find a snack if you get hungry. Neither of these things is necessarily bad in and of themselves, but if the routine becomes your autopilot for being bored, you may find yourself browsing endlessly or snacking unnecessarily without even realizing it.

The simplest solution is to ask yourself, "What do I do and why do I do it?" What is your autopilot for boredom, and why has that become your routine? You may conclude that your routine is good (when you're bored, you read a book or go for a run), and you want to continue doing so. You may come to the conclusion that your routine isn't so great (when you're bored, you spend hours scrolling social media and devouring a bar of chocolate).

You can use the Golden Rule to change your habits. You only need to make one change to the habit loop. Because you can't simply decide that you'll never be bored again (the cue), you'll need to change the part that matters (the routine) into something that still satisfies the need (reward). This is very simple once you've identified your habit loop, demonstrating the importance of self-reflection as a critical thinking skill. You ask yourself questions to figure out why you do something, then decide whether it's a habit you want to keep or abandon, and finally, pose yourself a new question to investigate... 'Will I still feel rewarded if I do 'X' instead?' The experimental phase is changing your habits.

After a few tries, you'll find one that works and fits your habit loop, and you'll conclude that it's your best new habit. You might get lucky and choose the best new routine the first time!

Just like with gene splicing, the goal is to remove the 'habit code' that you don't want and replace it with something you do.

Here are a few examples of common potential habit swaps:

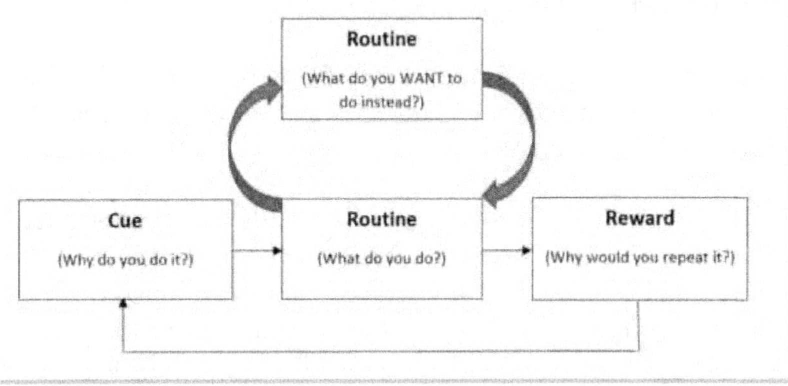

1. You're feeling low on energy (cue), so instead of eating chocolate (old routine), you opt for fruit (new routine). Both satisfy a sugar craving (reward), but the new routine is better for you.
2. You start work (cue), and instead of spending hours sorting emails (old routine), you make a to-do list of what you need to accomplish that day (new routine). Both satisfy the need to feel organized (reward), but the new routine ensures that you begin the day strategically rather than reactively.
3. You finish dinner and want to unwind (cue), so instead of immediately sitting down to watch TV (old routine), you clear your head while listening to an audiobook, music, or podcast you enjoy (new routine).
   Both satisfy the need for entertainment (reward), but the new routine indicates that you have finished tidying and can relax.
4. You get paid (cue), so instead of buying new clothes (old routine), you set aside the money for a specific desired item that you would not normally buy (new routine). Both still imply that your earnings are going towards a treat rather than bills (reward), but you will be saving for a more desired item.
5. You run out of toilet paper (cue), so instead of telling your partner (old routine), you immediately make a shopping list (new routine). Both give the impression that you have taken action, but the latter is more likely to avoid being caught short.
6. Instead of going out for a drink with friends after lunch on Sunday (cue), you go for a walk with friends (new routine). Both satisfy your social needs (reward), but the latter is healthier and more cost effective.

Buy one, get one free

Sometimes you'll want to incorporate a new habit that isn't a replacement for an old one. This is where you can practice 'habit stacking' or 'habit chaining.'

If your dentist advises you to floss your teeth, you will not abandon brushing in favor of flossing. By flossing every time you brush your teeth, you add flossing to your existing routine. It is much easier than trying to form a new flossing habit apart from brushing your teeth! Again, this is simple if you think of it as adhering to new habits to old

ones. It only takes a conscious decision to use your slow thinking'
mode to do it well.

If you want to start a new habit, you must make it simple to
maintain. Good habits are the easiest to establish. You may have
assumed that developing good habits necessitated a great deal of
dedication and willpower. Consider what a habit is: it is your autopilot,
so it does not require much thought or effort. It allows you to think
about other things. So consider when and how you can easily
incorporate a new habit into your existing routines, and you will be
successful with your changes.

Most routines can be completed at any time of day. Meditation,
journal writing, reading, and exercise can all be incorporated into your
daily routine. Writing my diary was always difficult for me because I
could do it whenever I wanted, which meant that I didn't have a set
time in my day for a long time.

It was frequently forgotten. I now write it right after my daughter
goes to bed; I've tied it to a fixed cue that occurs every day, and it's
now part of my routine, with minimal effort. The goal of habit stacking
is to achieve this. Check off several daily goals in the same session.

A quick list, such as the one below, is the quickest way to accomplish this.

Daily routines	New daily routines - pin to the existing ones

A daily list or a weekly list is an option. If you want to start a new daily habit, make a list of all the fixed routines you have in a day, such as making coffee, brushing your teeth, taking a shower, and so on. Try to list them in the order in which you usually do them. Then, on the other list, make a list of the routines you'd like to incorporate into your day.

Consider pinning each of the new habits to an existing routine to create a new, longer habit chain.

Make a list of weekly routines if you want to introduce new habits on some days of the week but not every day. It's possible that you'll only do a new routine on workdays, after a specific exercise class, or when you go shopping. List the activities that are regular and predictable but do not occur on a daily basis. Then, make a list of the new routines you want to incorporate and 'pin' each of them to the existing weekly routines.

Changes that are Small but Mighty

You now understand your habit loop and intend to either swap routines to improve your habits or pin a new routine on top of an existing good one.

Perhaps you'd like to upgrade some of your existing good habits to great ones. It may be tempting at this point to 'think big' and decide that your new routine will include a daily 10km run before breakfast. This is unlikely to be an effective goal unless you already run every morning. Remember that habits that stick are those that are simple to establish.

Voltaire famously said, "The best is the enemy of the good." It does not imply that you should lower your long-term goals, but doing something every day is preferable to doing something perfectly every once in a while. If you want to run 10km every morning, it is better to start with 2km rather than going out once a month to run 10km and then doing nothing on the other days.

A marathon training plan does not require you to run a marathon every time you go for a run. You begin slowly and gradually increase the amount of time and distance. You work on incremental improvements.

This method is well-known among inventors and scientists. It is rare to get the perfect result the first time when developing a new product. You modify it, test it, modify it again, and test it again. Things get better one step at a time. This is how everything from medicines to vacuum cleaners is created.

The 40th test experimental formula resulted in the successful product WD40. Similarly, James Dyson created 5,126 prototypes of his vacuum cleaner, all of which failed before the globally successful one that has made him millions. Each experiment involved determining which minor change could be made to improve the outcome. If the test was successful, the inventors made another minor change.

It's the same thing when it comes to changing your habits. If you want to end up with something brilliant, aim to make a lot of small, but significant, improvements. There are a few fundamental keystone habits to consider (more on that later), but the majority of your gains will come from small changes that add up to big changes. It's a snowball effect that makes bigger goals feel more tangible and closer.

For many years, the world of sports has been working with this theory. It was dubbed'marginal gains theory' by British cycling coach Dave Brailsford, who used it to improve everything from hand-washing to determining which parts of his team's bodies could be waxed. They got better results and more gold medals; the small gains added up. They were encouraged to look for 1% changes, and now technology allows for even more significant gains when new equipment becomes available.

New carbon footplates improve marathon runners' times by 2%, and in his sub-2-hour attempt, Eliud Kipchonge used a V-shaped formation of pace-setters designed by aerodynamics expert Robby Ketchell. So it pays to think outside the box and look for areas in your life where you can make small improvements.

A good place to start is to think about what saves us time, not just in the short term but also in the long term. How many times have you stated that you don't have enough time to do everything you want or need to do? However, we all have the same number of hours in a day. It is unchangeable. We only have control over how we use them. So making minor gains that save a few minutes is one way to make time' for other projects, or simply to relax without feeling guilty.

The following are examples of minor gains to make time':
1. Establish routines for shopping and meal planning so that you can make fewer trips.
2. Establishing cleaning routines to prevent chores from piling up and taking longer than necessary.
3. Creating routines that make the most of each trip out in order to reduce the number of hours spent traveling.
4. Establishing routines for checking emails and social media reduces the likelihood of wasting time stroking a phone screen.

5.   Establishing routines for storing and packing work or school bags to save time searching for misplaced items.

Saving money is another simple area where marginal gains can be applied. You can make minor financial gains by using various apps and simple comparison websites. If you chose the cheapest option, The savings would grow with each shopping trip. A traditional English proverb goes, "If you save the pennies, the pounds will save themselves," which perfectly sums up the concept of 1% gains.

You can think critically about what you really want to spend your money on and how you can do so in your current situation.

In business, this strategy is known as the Kaizen principle, which is a Japanese term that literally means 'constant improvement.' A series of logical marginal gains can significantly improve a company's productivity and effectiveness. The backbone saves time and money, but reducing physical waste directly affects these two, so what appears to be purely commercial has environmental credentials as well.

By optimizing your life, you will also benefit those close to you; consider how your relationships might benefit if you had more free time. What new ventures can you try, and what opportunities can you unexpectedly say 'yes' to?

What foundation has your life been built on?

Your foundational habits set the tone for the rest of your life. We can build entire portions of our lives on a rock or sand, as in the story and song "the wise man built his house upon the rock." The consequences of such minor decisions can be far-reaching. So figuring out what you're going to build your life on is the key to making rapid progress.

Hypocrites of Sleep

Anyone who has a small child understands the value of routine. Evidence suggests that bedtime routines improve sleep, behavior, and even parent-child relationships and language development. Many parents heed this advice and, as a result, adhere to a set routine. Even the youngest children can pick up on and be influenced by habits. Parents are aware of this and are taking steps to improve their children's outcomes. What about the adult routines, on the other hand?

We are much better at recognizing good and bad habits in others than we are at recognizing them in ourselves. We know that having a bedtime routine that includes no screen time, something relaxing to do, and a set 'lights out' time is beneficial. We all know that getting enough sleep allows us to think more clearly and make better use of our time.

Despite this, the World Health Organization has identified a 'sleep epidemic' that began in the Western world and is now widespread in Asia and Africa. So many of us ensure that our children get enough sleep while failing to establish similar routines for ourselves. Many of us are sleep deprivation hypocrites. Has 'Tired' ever been your default response when asked, 'How are you?' In many cultures, this is considered normal. Perhaps you believe that saying otherwise is a sign that you are not working hard enough. This is a widespread global issue.

You may have a number of objectives and targets in mind for bettering your life. Sleep is unlikely to be one of them. We ignore it. However, if you want to develop good habits and become a skilled critical thinker, this is where I recommend you start. Sleep is one of your most important habits, one on which your success is predicated.

Consider your bedtime routine for a moment. You may be able to get data on your waking hours, sleep length, and quality if you have a wearable smart device. You should aim for at least 7 hours of sleep per night. Every single night. Your bed and wake times should not vary significantly from day to day, which may be unavoidable if you work shifts, but it is something you can control in most professions. Be truthful in your analysis. Is it a solid enough foundation for the rest of your day?

Consider what you want that routine to be and what you don't want it to be. Work backward from the time you intend to sleep. Make some ground rules. When, for example, do you need to finish your work? What relaxes you and helps you sleep? This could include things like reading, yoga, meditation, journaling, or listening to music. You may already have a good idea or you may need to experiment.

You can apply the same logic to the start of your day. If you have a bad habit of oversleeping (keystone), getting up early in the morning can become a new keystone habit (routine) that can have a positive impact on other aspects of your life, such as eating breakfast every day without skipping it (routine), arriving at work on time (routine), and accomplishing more during the day (reward). This frequently coincides with going to bed late. Creating a new routine for either bedtime or waking up will make the other easier to change.

Adjust Your Morning Routine
Once you've analyzed your sleep, you can look at other keystone habits. Remember that keystone habits are small decisions that have a large impact on the rest of your day.

Consider some of your favorite childhood toys. Most people have fond memories of playing with Lego sets as children, and possibly as adults as well. It is an incredible tool for developing many skills, as you must sometimes follow instructions to achieve a specific end goal. If you fail to follow one of the early instructions precisely, the entire build may fail. It's possible you'll have to disassemble it and start over.

Some steps are easier to fix than others. Each project will have keystone steps.

The consequences of continuing with unchecked errors are not always obvious in our daily lives, but they are in another Lego venture. Lego has more options than ever before, including the ability to construct and program robots. The 'First Lego League' is an annual global competition for children to build robots that can complete specific tasks in two minutes. Robots must begin in one corner of a game mat, and players can only interact with them in that corner, so they require programming for directions. Even if the robot starts slightly off course, the errors add up as the robot moves across the mat. It ends up falling short of its objectives. Teams quickly discover that calibrating the robot at the outset is well worth their time. If the robot gets off to a good start, it will be able to go where they want it to go.

To avoid errors, we happily calibrate the technology around us. You most likely set all of your clocks to a known time, calibrate the scales in your bathroom or kitchen, and most of your smart electronic devices calibrate their location without your assistance.

What remains is for you to consider how to calibrate your day.

Calibration is the process by which we ensure that a device makes an accurate or true measurement. You are more complicated than a simple number to measure, but if you consider what you want to accomplish in a day as your true measurement, then good keystone habits will put you on the right track to achieving these goals. As a result, you must calibrate your day by establishing the proper starting point. Aside from sleep, consider what your daily success is built on.

Keystone habit number one is to get up early and consistently. This means a similar amount of time on workdays and days off if your job allows it.

Productivity is highest in the morning, and the most successful people have a morning routine. For most people, the adage "the early bird gets the worm" is more than just a saying. Even for teenagers, morning classes produce better test results than afternoon classes. Choose a time that allows you to do what you need to do that day while also allowing you to get enough sleep.

Keystone habit number two is to eat a nutritious breakfast. If this isn't already part of your morning routine, make it a priority. You have the option of making quick cereal, batch cooking, freezing low sugar muffins, or cooking something from scratch. According to research, a quick cereal-based breakfast option leads to 30-90 percent more micronutrient consumption throughout the day and lower fat intake.

Stay hydrated is a keystone habit (3). If you think you're hungry, make sure you're not just thirsty. If you are too stressed or busy to remember to drink, it is easy to become dehydrated. Water is the best way to rehydrate; coffee and tea are acceptable, but should not be your only sources. Improved hydration improves cognitive functions such as short-term memory, visual awareness, and mood. It is a simple thing to do well, so make it a habit!

The fourth and final pillar habit is to visualize and meditate. Meditation can take many different forms, such as prayer and yoga. The benefits of regular practice include reduced stress, depression, and anxiety throughout the day. The amount of time spent does not have to be significant, and you already know that less stress leads to better decision-making later on. Consider what that would mean for your work or personal relationships, or how you would appear in a presentation! This is an example of investing time now to save time later.

Exercise is a keystone habit (5). You don't have to go for a morning 10k run for this to work; there are plenty of apps and routines that are only 5-10 minutes long that can get your heart pumping and endorphins rising. Morning exercise may improve your immune function and academic performance because your brain is in a better state for learning and processing information.

Keystone habit (6): When performing minor tasks, ask yourself, "Why?"

Learn to pause and reflect. This is the first step toward better rational thought. What is it in the future that you will be grateful for doing or not doing? Slowing down and asking "Why?" is the foundation for the critical thinking habits you will develop.

Steps to Take

You can get a second opinion from a close friend or family member after you've gone over your existing habits, using the daily and weekly lists to identify known routines. Sometimes we have bad habits that we are unaware of but are obvious to others!

You can get feedback from another person in two ways to help you change your habits. For starters, they can act as your inquisition, assisting you in asking the difficult questions you may not want to ask yourself.

Second, they can serve as an accountability partner, helping to motivate you to stick with a new habit.

Inquisition

You can ask yourself these questions if you don't want to discuss them with someone else, but keep in mind that you may be biassed. If you see another person's opinion as a source of information rather than a source of criticism, you will be able to make more progress than you could on your own.

1. When attempting to replace a bad habit, what emotions are associated with the 'cue' and reward? Someone who wants to quit smoking may recognize the cue as going outside after work, but in order to identify an appropriate substitute, you must first identify the emotions that drive that choice.
2. Why do you want to change your habit in the first place? Even if it is for the benefit of another, you must find something that feels like a win for you. You may want to read more to demonstrate to your children that you are more literate, but reading will also improve your comprehension skills and broaden your knowledge. The selfish goal is also important for long-term success.
3. If you stick to a new habit, how can you reward yourself in ways other than the immediate reward in the habit loop? This is essentially a more sophisticated version of a sticker chart. There are numerous methods for tracking habits (see Chapter 5), but an ultimate reward is required to improve motivation, especially if you give up something you enjoy.
4. Who can help you, and how can they help you? Would you like to share your progress with someone else (as many apps allow), and if so, who? It may sound harsh, but it means you won't be able to hide your decisions and will have to face them. It functions similarly to a swear jar in terms of habit

tracking.

5. What technology can you use to help you remember? This could be a smartphone app or a post-it note. Even if they are well planned and simple to implement, new habits take time to establish. Reminders give you an advantage and free up your mind for other activities.

6. What will you do if things do not go as planned? You will have bad days, and anticipating them allows you to plan for them. A general rule is to avoid having two bad days in a row, so a 'miss one' day means you make an effort to do something important the next day.

7. What could go wrong and make you feel like you shouldn't try at all that day? Keep in mind that practice makes perfect. It is preferable to follow your new habit imperfectly but consistently than to do it perfectly or not at all.

8. Make a list of the habit swaps or stacks you want, then arrange them in the order you want them. What is your most important starting point? Do not attempt to complete all of them at once. You may have a sequence in place to gradually build a new habit to where you want it to be. You can also use this list as evidence of your progress. Take small steps. If you need more time for one habit, you must consider your other routines because there aren't any more hours in the day. Saying yes to one thing always means saying no to another! Make a list of your most important routines and plan around them.

Accountability

If you can enlist the help of a trusted companion, you will be able to establish a habit more quickly. Even better, sharing evidence that you have achieved your daily or weekly goal is an additional reward that makes it more appealing to achieve! According to an African proverb, " "If you want to travel quickly, go alone. Go together if you want to go far." " Habits are long-term goals; doing something for a few days does not constitute a habit. You are making plans for a better future.

So, what steps can you take to make accountability work for you?

1. Choose your partners wisely. It could be a friend, partner, coworker, or family member. They don't have to be an expert in the field you're pursuing; just someone who is concerned about your progress and will make checking in on you a priority. Children can be surprisingly effective accountability partners because you will want to set a good example for them by doing what you say you will do. If necessary, outsource. There's a reason why people pay to attend Slimming World classes rather than having their partners or friends check in on them. Personal trainers imply that you are held accountable for your physical progress. There are numerous businesses that can assist you in staying on track.
2. Be specific about the habit you want to maintain, how you intend to share it with them, and when you intend to update them.
3. Determine what will happen if you do not follow through on your commitments. Make certain that it is not judgmental and instead encourages you to get back on track. Something as simple as giving a small sum of money to a third party (not the accountability partner!) may suffice.
4. Go over a list of possible excuses with your accountability partner and plan what you'll say to each one. If you try to make excuses, you will only be hearing your own words back at you.

Once you're comfortable with using the habit loop and habit stacking to change your behavior, you can use it to achieve personal and professional objectives. You can also begin to apply it to skills and activities that actively promote the development of critical thinking. Good habits are not only the foundation for improved physical well-being and preventing you from eating the entire bag of popcorn, but they are also essential for mastering critical thinking techniques. The process of identifying the habit loop can become a habit in and of itself, and thus a tool that can be used with minimal effort.

Summary of the Chapter

Recognize and identify your autopilot habit loop in your daily life:
- What motivates you to do it? (Cue) What are you going to do? (routine) Why do you keep doing it? (reward)
- You can use the following strategies to change your habits:
- Use the Golden Rule: replace an old routine with a new routine while keeping the cue and reward intact, making the new routine simple to follow.
- Make a habit stack or habit chain by pinning a new routine into an existing habit - making the cue obvious.
- Make sure you understand how the change will benefit you directly and sell it to yourself - make the reason for the swap appealing.
- Make sure the reward still corresponds to your original desires and set up bigger rewards if you succeed in forming the new habit.
- Plan for marginal gains if you want to increase your returns. What can you do to improve by 1%? This also leads to more easily formed habits that grow over time.
- Determine your keystone habits in order to maximize the effectiveness of the rest of your day. These are frequently associated with :
- Sleep
- Nutrition
- Hydration
- Mindfulness
- Exercise

- Consider enlisting the help of an accountability partner for any changes you anticipate will be more difficult to implement. This can be someone you know well, a support group, or an app.

3
TURNING CRITICAL THINKING INTO A HABIT

"Time given to thought is the greatest time saver of all" - Norman Cousins

Finish the sentence 'If only I had the time...' Perhaps you would renovate your home, write a book, learn an instrument, socialize more, spend more time with your children instead of working on weekends, and go to the gym. What would you do if you had an extra hour each day?

That deepest desire is what you will make time for by training your autopilot to think critically without the use of a timer. Good habits save time while also lowering uncertainty and stress. So, by devoting some time to developing good critical thinking habits, you will have more time to do what you want in life.

You now have a framework for developing habits as well as the skills and characteristics required to improve your critical thinking ability. This chapter is about putting those two things together. When you make these into routines, you will notice a positive shift in how you think about and interact with the world.

Critical thinking habits entail more than simply strengthening and training your brain to think logically all of the time. They do, however, entail using more tools and techniques for thinking rationally in a habitual manner.

Adopting these habits allows you to keep your mind open and effectively deal with a wide range of problem-solving situations in your personal and professional life.

Why do we need to plan for these in advance? It all comes back to fast and slow thinking, to our autopilot in the twenty-first century. It is often easier to repeat the same thought patterns, just as it is easier to eat the same breakfast every day or order the same type of coffee every time. The new routine is not more difficult, but it does require some effort to create the mental space to consider a change.

Most people who do not think critically do so on purpose, believing that critical thinking requires more mental effort to establish new habits. It also necessitates self-reflection and accepting responsibility for your actions. Mastering critical thinking skills requires practice, and, like any other habit, this requires being consciously aware of the skill's need and then knowing what to do to acquire it.

Making Hobbies a Habit

Your goal is to become proficient in critical thinking. Just as putting on your shoes before leaving the house is a physical autopilot, the critical thinking skills discussed in Chapter 1 will serve as your mental autopilots. So, what routines should you incorporate into your daily habit loops to help you develop and master these skills?

You're probably at a different starting point for each hobby you want to turn into a habit. You'll need to either start a new hobby, incorporate it into an existing habit, or expand an existing habit to get more out of it. Consider your starting point for each habit in order to effectively incorporate it into your day.

Establish - this is for anything you haven't already done. Remember to start small, tying the new routine to an established habit. To establish it, you may need to use reminders, apps, accountability partners, or visual cues.

Embed - this is for a habit you already have but struggle to keep up with on a consistent basis. You should think about whether the routine is in the right place in your day or week, and you should unpick the habit loop to ensure you understand the cue and reward. You may need to remind yourself why you do it, or you may need to find a stronger reward or a more visible cue.

Extend - this is for an existing habit that you want to strengthen. You already have a habit loop in place that works well for you.

You must consider what else you wish to accomplish and how best to accomplish it. Do you need to invest more time, money, or change the substance of your routine? For example, you may read a lot but want to broaden your horizons by reading more widely. Change your routine to accommodate this. More on the various approaches in Chapter 4.

Read widely and frequently

"To develop the habit of reading is to build for yourself a refuge from almost all of life's miseries." Somerset, W. Maugham

Why?

Reading not only keeps you informed but also piques your interest and forces you to consider things from a variety of angles. It enables you to understand the various meanings of words and interpretations of ideas. Reading immerses you in another person's world, providing you with a fresh perspective and the ability to empathize with people you may never meet. It piques your interest, takes you to places you've never been, and teaches you how to communicate in situations you've never encountered before.

Literacy is essential for improving cognition 1 and promoting higher academic achievement. When you read more, you gain more knowledge, which allows you to analyze new problems because your cognitive load is reduced. You will naturally broaden your vocabulary as you learn more words and consider the deeper meaning of the text. The 'Matthew Effect' derives from the Bible's book of Matthew 25:29, which states, "For whoever has will be given more, and they will have an abundance." Whoever does not have, even what they do have, will have it taken away from them.'

This is true in many areas of life, but it is especially true in the acquisition of knowledge. Educators are paying close attention to this because there are still significant socioeconomic gaps in academic outcomes that are linked to varying parental literacy levels. 2. Regardless of your background, it is never too late to begin developing a reading habit. It is always advantageous.

How?

This is determined by your starting point and your objectives. Is it necessary to establish, embed, or extend the habit? Do you always intend to read but never get around to it? Do you read infrequently and want to make it a habit rather than a pastime? Do you already read a lot but want to broaden your horizons? Do you enjoy reading but want to delve a little deeper into text analysis?

1. If you don't read books often but want to start, choose a topic you'd like to learn more about or ask a friend with similar tastes to recommend a book. It makes no difference whether you begin with fiction or nonfiction. You can buy a new or used book, borrow one from a friend, or visit a library. Reading can be a very inexpensive habit! If you're still unsure about which book to start with, look at the New York Times bestseller list or search for popular books online.
2. If you prefer nonfiction in bite-sized chunks, look into newspaper or magazine subscriptions. Most are available in both electronic and traditional paper formats. Using social media may be appealing. Nonetheless, the quality of language is frequently lower at a much younger reading age. Furthermore, algorithms operate in such a way that you may find yourself in an echo chamber, where accessing opposing viewpoints can be difficult.
3. If you have a lot of reading material but most of it is unread, choose something that will be a quick win. Moby Dick is probably not the best choice in this situation.
4. Participate in a book club. If you don't know of any, there are plenty of online options. Alternatively, organize one with friends, family, or coworkers. Book clubs are excellent for improving reading habits because you are told what to read and when to read it, and you have ready-made accountability partners who will notice if you haven't finished. You are also more likely to read material that you would not have chosen on your own.
5. Place the reading material where you intend to read it. Place a book on your pillow when you wake up in the morning or by the sofa before you leave for work. If you use a digital device, make sure your routine includes charging it. Nothing puts a halt to a good reading habit like an e-reader that frequently runs out of battery power.
6. If you are short on time, audiobooks can be a great option. Multitasking is rarely successful, but this is one of the exceptions; you can listen to an audiobook while doing physical tasks and benefit from it. Listen while doing housework, gardening, commuting to work, or going for a run. However, in order to listen

properly, you must ensure that you are not reading or talking at the same time. You can't listen while reading or talking and understand what you're hearing. Although audiobooks provide the book's content, they do not provide the word recognition that seeing the written form provides, so if you want to improve your use of written language, it is best to stick to visual media.

Take Note of It

"Just write every day for the rest of your life." Read carefully. Then watch what happens. "The majority of my friends who are on that diet have very pleasant jobs." Ray Bradbury's

Why?

Writing, in conjunction with reading, teaches us how to think. Many experts would also argue that writing IS thinking and that it assists us in distinguishing between what we know and what we think we know, as well as in seeing and evaluating our thoughts more clearly. That's a quick way to improve your self-reflection and communication skills. You first learn to write, and then you write to learn. 3. You learn about yourself, your opinions, your feelings, and your decision-making process. When you put something in writing, you have the opportunity to be truthful and track changes and attitudes over time. All of these abilities make it easier to be aware of your habits and make more informed decisions about the best next step for you.

How?

Consider whether you need to establish, embed, or extend this habit. Do you only write emails on a daily basis? Do you keep a journal on vacation but not as part of your regular routine? Do you keep a journal on a regular basis but want to be more analytical? Do you prefer to write on paper, on a tablet, or by typing?

1. If you want to keep a diary but are intimidated by the many blank pages, look for a 5-year diary with very short sections for each day. Choosing a pre-dated version helps structure the diary and allows you to easily fill it with limited space. You don't have to wait until

January 1st; there are plenty of customizable diaries where you can choose the start date.

2. Journals with a specific purpose, such as a gratitude, prayer, health, or exercise journal, are alternative activities that can introduce a quick daily writing habit. This can be combined with another habit you want to develop - keeping an exercise journal can assist you in developing a better exercise habit. Again, there are plenty of appropriate headings for various activities available to buy or print at home to help prompt you.

3. Push writing a little further by allowing for more open-ended pieces. Create a profile of yourself. This is a self-reflective task, not a self-centered one. This could be for your benefit or the benefit of another. You can write about your vacations or how you developed your career so that you will have stories to read in the future. You can write about your childhood in order to record stories for your children to hear. When my brother married, his wife received a short book about him titled 'An idiot's guide to guiding an idiot.' It goes without saying that neither are idiots, but the idea of writing a 'how to guide about yourself or someone close to you can be very revealing and a more humorous way of writing. If that feels too personal, try writing a "how-to" guide about your pet or a hobby.

4. Write some letters or articles for magazines, platforms, or newspapers that you read if you want to improve your ability to communicate with an audience. It will cause you to reconsider your choice of words and tone of delivery, with the added benefit of the possibility of receiving a more obvious reward than simply the satisfaction of having communicated your thoughts.

5. If you already have a strong self-reflective writing habit, you can combine writing with research to create a piece about a specific location, topic, or person. This could be one you're already familiar with or one you'd like to learn more about. You can do this for yourself or with the goal of publishing in mind. Set a reasonable time or word limit for yourself each day.

Create Systems to Help You Achieve Your Goals

"You do not reach the level of your ambitions. You are reduced to the level of your systems. Your desired outcome is your goal. Your system is a set of daily habits that will get you there." - Mr. James Clear

Why?

Running a marathon is a common 'bucket list' goal. You almost certainly have friends who have done or have discussed doing this.

Some people do it, enjoy it, and then repeat the process. Most people do it once, get the T-shirt, and then settle for more sensible runs.

Marathons are popular because they have a clear and obvious goal. Something to cross off the to-do list. Telling yourself you're training for a marathon sounds good. Running a marathon, on the other hand, is not the best way to develop a good running habit. Your focus is on the goal, and you may become concerned about your time, how you will avoid injury in the preceding runs, and how others will judge you. When we set lofty goals, we set ourselves up for massive failures.

This can cause anxiety or a mental block, which is not what you want when trying to make progress in your life!

Goals aren't inherently bad, but they aren't the key to successful habit formation. Instead, you should concentrate on systems. Micro-changes that occur in the background are referred to as systems. If your goal is to run a marathon, you will not develop a running habit by accident. You are much more likely to complete a marathon if you develop a running habit. The presence of a good system results in the achievement of the goal.

When you focus your attention on a system, you set yourself up for success in small increments throughout the day rather than worrying about the failure of one final task. You are succeeding by going on daily runs, and the marathon is merely a byproduct, not the defining feature. It also means that if an event is canceled (hello, 2020), or if you become ill or injured, you will not feel as if you have failed to achieve your goal. The new goal is the system that leads to a habit that lasts beyond race day.

How?

First and foremost, consider whether you need to Establish, Embed, or Extend this habit. Are you a 'goals-oriented' person who craves the rush of a big win? Do you think the practice and preparation phases are just as important as the main event? Do you measure your success in terms of daily routines or one-time events? How much research do you conduct before making a major decision?

1. Make a list of your current objectives. What system is required to support that goal? Without the goal as your focal point, you can figure out what habits need to be established or embedded to get you to your goal. Tracking your habits and rewarding yourself for sticking to your plan can be your new 'goal' and source of achievement.
2. Think about specific aspects of your life. Have you considered changing careers? You may have a gut feeling about this, but in order to critically approach the issue, you must shift your focus from the goal of a new career to the development of systems that pave the way for it. Instead of simply aiming to change careers because you want to, you can use different thinking processes such as researching (on the new career you are considering), questioning (asking people in the same career you want to have) and comparing views (reconciling the opinions of various people you talk to).

Check Again And Question Yourself
"Often, the most difficult questions are the ones to which we secretly know the answers." What are you fleeing? "What are you looking forward to?"
Sanhita Baruah's

Why?
Have you ever wished you could live a few parallel lives to see which choices work best for you? Or maybe you could go back in time and make a different decision with the benefit of hindsight? While there is no foolproof way to make big decisions in the future, you can develop habits to reduce the chances of making a mistake.

You don't just question others to gather evidence. Questioning yourself is one of the most powerful habits you can cultivate.

Not in a negative way that encourages self-doubt, but in a positive way that reassures you that you have exhausted all possibilities in your search for the best option.

Apply critical thinking to yourself: question arguments, actions, facts, and ideas; test or counter your arguments and thoughts until you have the strongest argument based on your knowledge.

How?
Do you need to establish, embed, or expand your habit of questioning?

Do you make important decisions by asking others what they think you should do rather than asking yourself? Do you ever stop yourself from considering a different outcome just to make your life easier? Do you already use questioning but need to consider the weighting of the 'evidence' you gather?

1. Consult with others, but also with yourself. When you are under pressure, it is common to ask someone you trust to make decisions for you, and then you compile evidence to support their decision. Make sure you first ask yourself.

2. Be a little selfish from time to time. It is critical to consider how your decision will affect others, but you must also consider how they will affect you. You will be sorry if you choose something that makes everyone else happy but makes you unhappy, no matter how much you love those other people. 5. You should ask yourself why you want to do what you want to do.

3. When faced with a major decision, apply De Bono's Thinking Hats concept. 6. This entails approaching a decision or problem from six different angles. It's a great way to make sure you've covered all of your bases before finalizing your strategy. The six hats are as follows:

- The White 'Objective' Hat - Only looking for facts and figures, with no bias or emotion.
- The Red 'Emotive' Hat - Only Emotions
- The 'Cautious' Black Hat identifies potential dangers or weaknesses.
- The Yellow 'Optimistic' Hat - Thinking positively and hoping for the best.
- The Green 'Creative' Hat: Where could it lead, and what new opportunities might it open up?
- The Blue 'Organized' Hat - Overview of the process and evidence organization.

4. Seek adversity and take on the role of the Devil's advocate. You can enlist a trusted friend to help you with this as long as they don't start offering their opinions. Pit yourself against yourself on purpose. Make a list if necessary.

5. Think about having coaching sessions. Coaching is not the same as mentoring; it is someone else asking you questions that help you narrow down what you truly think and feel. This can be useful if you need to make a big decision and you don't want to make it in front of people you know. A coach is objective and will not steer you in any particular direction to achieve your goal.

6. Refuse to conform to what others expect of you. Feel at ease deviating from the expected structure, learning to defy the rules, or breaking free from your previous understanding in order to discover what is true and rational. Have you ever had someone expect you to do a certain job, live in a certain type of house, have a certain number of children, and have your life look the way they expect it to by a certain age?

How many of your decisions have been your own, rather than what others expected you to do? This is not to say that you should defy any familial or societal expectations; many have logical foundations, but you should question them and determine if they truly apply to you at this time. Be a critical thinker who never accepts anything at face value.

Look for Good Conversations

"Ideas are discussed by great minds." Events are discussed by ordinary people. "Small minds debate people," said Eleanor Roosevelt.

Why?

There is a reason why gossip magazines are so popular. It takes very little effort to make a passing remark about someone's dress size or the color of their new car. Passing on observations is a natural part of being human, but it is easy, and a conversation about a celebrity's love life is unlikely to challenge our thinking.

This lack of substantive conversation is ingrained in popular culture.

Films can now be subjected to the Bechdel–Wallace test, which assesses how women are portrayed in fiction. The test was inspired by an Alison Bechdel cartoon in which women discuss their movie-choice rules. Their guidelines are as follows:

1) the film must feature at least two women who converse with each other,
2) the film must be about something other than a man, and
3) the film must be about something other than a man.
It is now also necessary for the women to be named characters.

Approximately 60% of films pass this test, and many of them do so solely because women are talking about marriage and babies. There's nothing wrong with these harmless conversation starters, but they don't encourage a variety of discussions.

If you look at greeting cards, you will notice the topics that society expects us to discuss. Women, it appears, should talk about their families, flowers, and cakes. Men, it appears, should talk about sports and automobiles.

Having conversations that go beyond people and objects is valuable to us all because it gives us the feeling that we can transcend age and gender divides in our verbal interactions.

Conversations are about more than just exchanging ideas and sharing dreams. Finally, it can help to improve deep listening, impactful learning, and action planning. Seek to comprehend before being comprehended. A good conversation should cause us to reconsider both others and ourselves. It should encourage us to think more broadly and wisely.

Conversations can help us clear up misunderstandings, clarify our intentions in order to prompt action, and improve our empathy. To that end, we must go beyond discussing individuals and events.

How?

Is it necessary for you to Establish, Embed, or Extend this habit? Do you have more text conversations than face-to-face conversations? Do you see meetings as a chance to gather information or simply to share information? Do you recall and reflect on previous conversations?

1. Make time in your personal life for conversation, whether face to face or virtually. If necessary, you can add this as a new routine pinned to an existing habit. You might decide to have a family video call after Sunday lunch, or you might make a point of talking with those you live with over breakfast without the distractions of phones or television. You could walk with a colleague to get lunch and talk on the way, or you could jog with a friend to catch up.

2. Consider who you speak with on a regular basis. Are you exposed to a variety of viewpoints, or are you only exposed to an echo chamber? Try striking up a conversation while waiting in line, for a bus, or with someone at work you pass by frequently but rarely speak with. Aim to speak to people of various ages and from various cultural backgrounds. Even brief conversations can leave an impression.

3. Unplug your computer on a regular basis. While it is convenient to listen to a podcast, audiobook, or relax with some music during a commute or shopping trip, it is also an opportunity to observe and interact with others.

Make a plan for a well-balanced approach. If you go around with your earphones in and don't speak to anyone, you should think about the opportunities for a conversation you're passing up.

4. Spend time talking to children. Most people will be delighted to tell you about their latest obsession. It is an excellent way to hone your listening skills while also providing real value to the child. Many children are overlooked in conversation, but if you take the time to talk with them, they can provide remarkably astute observations.

5. Make plans to speak with people of an older generation as well. They have witnessed significant changes and can be an invaluable source of information and perspective. Consider family, neighbors, or people you see while out and about.

6. Make plans to have more in-depth conversations with some of your closest friends and family members. When we meet others, we frequently cover superficial details, and the high, like a sugary snack, does not last long. Substantive conversations entail more than just the weather and what you're having for dinner. Try to shift your focus from people to events, and then to ideas. If you're stuck for ideas, look up a list of conversation starters online.

When It Is Necessary, Change Your Opinion

"Progress is impossible without change, and those who are unable to change their minds will be unable to change anything." -G. Bernard Shaw

Why?

Another habit that improves critical thinking is changing our minds or making different decisions in the face of new information. This does not imply that you should be insecure about the way you think of the decisions you make. It is about being open-minded, accepting when you are mistaken, and repositioning yourself as needed. It is a matter of putting accuracy and truth ahead of your ego.

We live in an information-rich world. You can conduct extensive research and still discover that new evidence emerged after you made your decision, causing your conclusion to change.

Scientists must constantly do this; without people who discover and accept new evidence, there would be very little technological progress in our world. Critical thinkers see this habit of making decisions as open cases rather than closed cases as a positive that leads to better outcomes, rather than a flaw in their abilities. It is a more difficult habit to develop than it appears! To master it, you must be more concerned with getting it right than with being correct.

How?
Is it necessary for you to Establish, Embed, or Extend this habit? Above all, this habit is often motivated by personal pride. Changing our minds is viewed as a weakness by some and is undervalued in society.

How do you feel when you have to change your mind about something? Are you grateful or frustrated if someone presents you with new information that contradicts your previous conclusions? The extent to which you cling to previous decisions indicates how well you have already developed this mental habit.

1. Try to think of your decisions as 'a decision,' rather than my decision.'
   1. When new evidence emerges, changing your mind feels less personal, and your ego is less likely to interfere.
   2. Assume you are making a decision for a friend or relative. What would you suggest they do?
   3. It can be difficult to change our minds when it means deviating from a path we've already charted. As in the previous example, it is much easier to go back down the path and choose the correct path than to continue on the wrong one. The time spent correcting yourself in the short term is likely to be less significant than the long-term impact of the wrong decision.

Choose the future you will be grateful for.

4. Approach the decision as if it were a scientific experiment or a legal case.
5. If new evidence became available, scientists and lawyers would be expected to revise their positions. The same is true for your life choices. There are very few decisions that are truly final.
6. Identify your excuses and ask yourself if you made them defend a point of view that needs to be reconsidered.

Avoid Making Hasty Conclusions

"I learned to be patient enough to listen when people express their opinions, even if I disagree with them." "You can't reach a fair decision in a dispute unless you listen to both sides," Nelson Mandela said.

Why?

To become an expert critical thinker, you must train yourself not to jump to conclusions, especially in the absence of data. It is a deliberate effort to consider various information and aspects of a problem, issue, or situation before making a decision.

Nelson Mandela mastered the art of decision-making and leadership through respect. Someone asked him, "How did you become such a good leader?" "Because I was the last to learn to speak," Mandela replied. He had grown up in a household where the decision-maker listened to the opinions of others before entering the discussion.

He saw the leader's role as "forming a consensus rather than telling people what to do." "Don't enter the debate too early," he advised others.

At the end of a meeting, he would summarise points and subtly steer it to what he believed led to the best decision, even if this differed from his original opinion.

How?

Consider a situation in which you had to make a significant decision, not just which movie to watch next. This will assist you in determining whether you need to Establish, Embed, or Extend this habit. Do you usually decide what you want to do first and then persuade others? Do you conduct a quick check for information, but only from sources that will support your original ideas? Do you thoroughly vet some decisions but leave others to chance because you're too tired or it takes too long?

1. You can gather unbiased information by listening to others before speaking. By conducting research prior to expressing your opinions, you can avoid acting on stereotypes, emotions, or taking the path of least resistance without considering alternatives. Listen first and speak last, as Mandela did.

2. When faced with a decision, ask yourself what the most obvious answer is, and then ask yourself why. Is it because that is the decision that others expect you to make? If that's the case, who is expecting you to make that decision? Could you provide evidence to your future self to back up your decision?

3. Make a list of situations in which you frequently make rash decisions. Make a list of options. It is sometimes easy to predict when you will need to make a decision, but it is difficult to conduct the research. For example, during a job interview, you'll need to make assumptions about the team you'd be working with, the location, and the role. Some preparation can be done ahead of time, but some evidence must often be gathered on the day. However, you can prepare ahead of time the appropriate questions to ask about the workplace or the team. Due to a lack of solid information, it is easier to make better decisions without relying on gut feelings and stereotypes.

Steps to Take

Determine your starting point for each critical thinking skill. To organize your thoughts, you could use a grid-like the one below.

Critical Thinking Habit	Establish it by...	Embed it by...	Extend it by...
Reading			
Writing			
Building systems			
Questioning yourself			
Seeking good conversations			
Changing your opinions			
Not jumping to conclusions			

Make an honest assessment of what you already do and plan how you will continue to grow that habit in the short, medium, and long term by committing to specific steps. Choose which one to work on first. Rome was not built in a day, but rather by laying bricks one at a time. You can create excellent new mental auto-pilots that will save you time and effort in the long run when navigating the world.

As with physical habits, consider using a habit tracking app or chart. Aim to establish, embed, and extend critical thinking habits over time. Determine your starting points for each habit in order to progress toward your new autopilots.

Habits to cultivate include:
- Daily and extensive reading
- Writing
- Creating systems to achieve goals
- Doubt-checking and self-questioning
- Having fruitful discussions
- Changing your mind when necessary
- Avoiding hasty conclusions
- Using the habit loop and pinning them to existing habits, plan for the habits.

4
MAKE IT STICK TODAY, TOMORROW, AND NEXT YEAR

"Habit is a cable; we weave a thread of it each day, and at last we cannot break it" - Horace Mann

Assume you're in the market for a new car. It is free of blemishes, clean, and runs smoothly. And you want it to stay that way. You wash it every weekend, don't eat or drink inside, and vacuum the seats and carpets. You double-check the fluid levels and the electrics. Before each long drive, you check the tyre pressure.

Fast forward five years, and you're still driving the same car. Do you take care of your older car in the same way you do your new one? Do you clean it, inspect it, and protect it as much as you can?

If we allow it, habits change over time. Even the most ingrained habits can fade away over months or years if no conscious effort is made to maintain them. This is why children excel at cleaning up after a new pet, adults excel at setting aside time to get to know a new date, and anyone can commit to a new workout routine or hobby for a few months. When the novelty of a situation wears off, you must embed a habit that you have begun to establish.

Getting It to Stick

Life changes and your habit cues may shift as a result. You change jobs, and the gym you used to go on your way home every day is no longer on your route, so you don't go. You have a baby, and your new morning routine requires you to skip brushing your teeth.

Even if your circumstances change, you must make a conscious effort to maintain your current habits. This chapter discusses how to keep habits going overtime to keep them from becoming stale and to help you feel the benefits so strongly that even when your life changes, you keep the habits going.

Organize Your Work

How do you go about doing your grocery shopping? Do you make a shopping list or just go to the store when you realize you're about to run out of food? What you do here reveals a great deal about your overall organizational levels.

If you get a little organized, you can save time and avoid wasting money and food. Plan your meals for the week and create a shopping list that includes what you don't already have on hand. On busy days, batch cooking allows you to have leftovers ready. Best of all, by implementing organizational habits like this to streamline daily tasks, you free up time and mental space for other things.

It's difficult to get excited about meal planner sheets, but the benefits of avoiding last-minute meal panic, extra take-out bills, and late-night shopping trips for essentials are worth celebrating.

Putting a semblance of order on tasks and assigning them a priority level is a great way to streamline a hectic day. We are often able to accomplish more when we have a sense of order.

Because developing good critical thinking habits entails organization and prioritization, try making use of lists on busier days.

A life planner, which combines a diary and a to-do list, is an easy way to accomplish this. You can easily fit monthly, weekly, or daily tasks into your schedule. If you have household tasks that need to be completed, this allows for shared viewing and usage.

Planning when pets are cleaned, bins are emptied, and other minor tasks save you time and mental space. Get your house in order so you can get your mind in order. Various methods, such as the 'KonMarie' method of tidying or the Team TOMM housework plan, can also help guide you in organizing the mundane aspects of life and giving you back your thinking space and time.

When your daily necessities are in order, you can deal with change more effectively. You'll have less chaos to distract you from the new critical thinking habits you're trying to establish.

Work On Both Your Mind And Your Body

Consider the most recent application form you completed. Whether it's for a University course or a job application, chances are the form will ask about extracurricular activities. It's not just grades or previous roles. No one wants to hire a slacker, but even fewer want to hire someone who has no life outside of work or school. It may appear to be a good idea to refuse all social events in order to further your studies or work late, but a balance is required to avoid burnout.

You can plan your life down to the minute, but your heart isn't always in it. There will be days when you are more energized and joyful than others. This is normal and does not constitute a failure. Know your limits and don't push yourself too far. You can calculate how much time you need for sleep, social interaction, exercise, spirituality, and quietness in order to think clearly. This is unique to each individual. Make a concerted effort to determine your limits, and then ensure that your daily plans allow for this.

Maintaining a broader perspective in life will aid in the development of tolerance, open-mindedness, and overall empathetic behavior. Your new habits will be easier to maintain if you do not feel exhausted or if you are sacrificing something important to your well-being. Choosing to forego a workout in order to read more is not the goal, and it is unlikely to be beneficial to you.

Discover your true passion, reason, purpose, or goal.

What would you do with your life if you could do anything you wanted? Would you do more of what you're already doing or change course entirely? Everything you do, especially your habits, should be intentional and lead to the life you want. When everything you do, including how you think, is based on what you enjoy doing and what you want to achieve, habits like critical thinking become second nature.

Perhaps you enjoy working with young students and leading career workshops. You realize you have a strong desire to reach out to and assist others, which gives you a sense of accomplishment. You are well aware that you would be more effective in that role if you consistently practiced rational thinking, good questioning, active listening, and other critical thinking skills. When you actively link developing these skills to the ideal role, you've added another reward to the habit loop. The habit is about your future potential as well as the potential of others.

This also applies to personal relationships. Your most important goal may be to fulfill your role as a parent or as a partner. There are clear advantages to not jumping to conclusions, being fair-minded and humble, and developing clearer communication skills in your personal relationships and professional goals. The fact that critical thinking habits have a positive impact on all aspects of your life and are not limited to one'season' of life is why they are important to cultivate.

Take the initiative and accept responsibility.

'The dog ate my homework isn't just a make-believe excuse. It is on a list of many different reasons for a lack of work produced on time, some of which are most likely true and some of which are most emphatically not. Teachers hold far more regard for students who admit to not having completed the work and devise a plan to rectify the situation than for those who try to avoid any blame or responsibility. Students who make excuses on a regular basis are unlikely to succeed.

Critical thinkers, like everyone else, make mistakes in their decision-making process. To keep any habit, physical or mental, you must avoid making excuses. If you miss a day, learn from your mistake and recover quickly. If you make excuses a habit, they will become the routines you follow. You end up giving up before you've even begun.

Improve Your Self-Discipline And Willpower

These two abilities are possibly the most fundamental and important in habit change and formation. Willpower is a sudden and fleeting burst of focused energy, whereas self-discipline is structured, well-thought-out, and consistent.

The marshmallow test, developed in 1972, demonstrates how this begins at a young age and has been used to track self-discipline from childhood to adulthood. A marshmallow on a plate was shown to preschoolers.

They were free to eat it if they so desired. They could eat that one and get a second one if they could wait 10 minutes. Even 30 years later, test success rates correlated with future success and improved health. Children were more successful at self-discipline when they had to work together to achieve the goal. Accountability, it turns out, works from a very young age!

According to research, self-control is one of the most important predictors of success, both personally and academically. To be able to resist distractions and temptations that could derail your habits, practice small acts of self-control each day (when to stop eating cookies or when to put down your phone).

Surround Yourself with Thinkers Who Are Critical

You may have heard Jim Rohn's adage that "you are the average of your closest five friends." Perhaps you've checked with your closest friends, and they appear to be in good shape... There are no bad habits to try to derail yours. This is a good start, but sometimes simple rules are overly simplistic; the impact on your life extends beyond your small close circle of friends to people you see only occasionally and even those you have never met.

It turns out that if your friends' friends gain weight, begin smoking, or become less happy, the ripple effect spreads. Even if you have never met them, you are more likely to gain weight, smoke, or be unhappy. The influence of your immediate and extended social circles on your life is quantifiable.

How can you use this to help you establish new habits? You can collaborate with existing friends to achieve common goals, use them as accountability partners, and, if necessary, consider expanding your social network to include those who already have these skills. Spending a lot of time with critical thinkers helps you train your mind to think like them, just as spending time with friends who read widely encourages you to try new literature.

Stay away from overthinking.

Have you ever found yourself staring at the 'Loading' screen while waiting for a video, upload, or update to begin? We can become engrossed in our thoughts in the same way that we can become engrossed in looking at a screen for no apparent reason. Consider it a mental traffic jam. Thinking clearly is beneficial and will help you get to your destination more quickly.

When you try to do this during rush hour, you will overthink.

Critical thinkers tend to think more deeply, avoiding the so-called analysis paralysis and information overload.

You, too, can avoid this stumbling block, just as you can avoid getting stuck in traffic if you carefully plan your journey time and route.

The first thing to try if you get stuck in your head is to bring yourself back into the room. This is useful for anxiety and overthinking, as well as any time you need to re-establish your connection to reality. Use the 5-4-3-2-1 method: pay attention to five things you can see, four things you can touch, three things you can hear, two things you can smell, and one thing you can taste.

You can refocus on the task at hand once you're 'back in the room.' This frequently goes hand in hand with planning, as we can become overwhelmed if we try to multitask or complete tasks in absurdly short time frames. Remember to only do one thing at a time, and to identify what that thing is and why you're doing it. Usually, focusing on embedding one habit at a time will suffice.

Sometimes all you have to do is 'do the next right thing.'
When overthinking persists and becomes a habit, you can use other skills to help you figure out what's causing it. It can help to write it down or talk it through. Going for a run, a walk, or reading can help you clear your mind. Take note of what works for you in order to find a constructive way to deal with your worries or negative thoughts.

Perfect Practice Makes Perfect
Any habit must be instilled through repetition. Don't aim for perfection.

Plan for practice, and 'perfect' may follow. If a couple wants to have a child, it is better for them to... 'practice' rather than spend hours calculating the odds each day to try only once when they believe the conditions are ideal.

Habits are, by definition, recurring events, not one-time occurrences.
They are not a 'one shot to get it right,' and many people fail to establish habits if they expect each day to be perfect. Accept flaws and give it your all every day if you want to establish a habit for the long haul.

Simple Steps for Developing Critical Thinking Habits
Make Reading a Habit

Set aside thirty minutes each day to read and compare the news from at least three different sources:
1. Make a list of the most important takeaways from each news site.
2. Examine what they have in common (if they're telling the same story) and where they diverge.
3. Examine what you've learned from them.
4. Look for additional related information if you believe something is still missing.
5. Form your own opinion on the subject.

Create a Writing Habit

Set aside sometime each day to write in a journal, either physical or electronic.
1. Identify key events in your day; think about what you might find significant when you read it later.
2. Each day, jot down key insights from news and articles you've read in your own words.

Maintain a development diary for your professional and/or personal life.
1. Keep a separate journal entry for each problem situation you encounter, whether major or minor, the steps you took to approach the problem, and the outcome (e.g., whether the problem was resolved or remains unresolved).
2. Go over your journal on a weekly basis and identify your thought patterns, failures, and small victories.
3. Examine your patterns and use what you learn to make positive changes. Other habits may change as a result of your writing. Instill the habit of systems (rather than goals).

Extend your day's physical system setups. Use what you've learned about laying out systems of thought to improve your other critical thinking skills.

Consider 'soft' goals like feeling more thankful, relaxed, and happy. Create systems that will help you achieve your 'feeling' goals. This is frequently much more difficult than systems for achieving physical goals.

1. Identify the factors that contribute to your 'soft' goals, such as spending time with family, going for walks outside, or engaging in a hobby.
2. Pick a goal that is simple for you to achieve. For example, you could choose to take three deep breaths before responding to a difficult email or phone call to improve your emotional control and, as a result, make you feel more relaxed when dealing with difficult situations.
3. Make a list of actions you could take to improve the level of this 'soft' goal in your life.

Make the systems a topic of conversation at work or at home; explain to others what you are aiming for by shifting your focus. This way, you can solidify the reasoning behind your systems while also receiving support.

1. Select a phrase that explains your focus succinctly. Make it clear to yourself and others that you are focusing on practice rather than perfection.
2. Without referring to the goal, write down the reasons why your system is beneficial.
3. Put these reasons somewhere you can easily see or find them.
4. Discuss the reasons for the system rather than the motivation for the goal with your family, friends, or colleagues.

Instill a Questioning Habit

When you have a big decision to make, take some time to weigh your options, either aloud or in writing.

1. Intentionally include options that you would normally dismiss; one should keep the status quo as a comparison (or 'control' if you are scientific).
2. Make a list of the pros and cons for each one.

3. Seek input from others on potential solutions; they may have ideas you haven't considered.
4. Summarize and rank each option.

If you have more time before making a decision, write down your reasons for your decision every day.

1. Try to come up with a new reason to justify your choice each time.
2. Identify potential reasons for making a different decision. This will assist you in thinking more broadly.
3. When appropriate, try out some of these alternatives.
4. Examine your options and reasoning. Have you discovered that you've been stuck in a rut or that you've passed up some great opportunities?

Make a list of questions to ask yourself in key locations, such as 'why...?' These can serve as reminders for other habits while also encouraging you to double-check your decisions as a good mental habit.

1. A note taped to your phone charger could read, 'Why do you want to look at social media right now?'
2. A note on your refrigerator could read, 'Why do you want a cookie right now?'

Instill a Deep Conversation Habit

Find a news site that covers current events that interest you.

1. Identify a friend or relative with whom you would be willing to discuss the topic; they may already be knowledgeable in that field.
2. Actively plan a time each week or fortnight to talk with them about articles you've both read.
3. Maintain an open conversation with no agenda. Take the time to listen to what they have to say.

Find out when the town hall and council meetings are taking place in your area. There will be a wide range of people with whom you can discuss policy and principles.

1. Make a note of the dates in your calendar so you can commit to attending.
2. Identify anyone else who might be able to accompany you. This will make you feel more at ease if you are in a new situation and will also serve as accountability for your attendance.
3. Prepare ahead of time by reading up on the topics to be discussed.
4. Plan ahead of time which questions you want to be answered.
5. Make a plan to listen to those who have opposing views and aim for conversations rather than arguments.

Make a Habit of Having Diverse Opinions

Choose a major news story, such as climate change, trade, gun control, or taxes.

1. Follow the story over time and write down your thoughts on it.
2. Take note of how the evidence alters your feelings.
3. Recognize the opinions of others close to you or the current political situation.
4. Examine your opinions over time; if they haven't changed, why not? What evidence changed your mind if they did?
5. Determine what evidence is required to change your mind and do not hesitate to seek it.

Choose a minor point of view that you are willing to investigate.
Perhaps you avoid a particular type of food because you believe you dislike everything?

1. Use examples to see if your opinion is still valid or if you just had a bad experience that tainted your perception.
2. Plan to expand your testing as needed.
3. Keep a journal entry identifying the point at which you changed your mind and why.

Incorporate A Forming Fair Conclusions Habit

When you read or watch news stories, unpick them.

1. What conclusion are they attempting to persuade the reader to reach? We frequently jump to conclusions because we are led there by others or the media.
2. What sources were used? Why? Learn to recognize when a source is leading you down their path rather than allowing you to choose your own.
3. Determine whether additional evidence is required and make a list of publications that lack this rigor.

Experiment with your pals. People's conclusions are influenced by what they define as "the best," but our definitions of what is best vary greatly.

1. Ask yourself and others what they look for in a good house, car, partner, job, vacation, and so on.
2. Examine the responses, especially your own and those of those close to you.
3. What different conclusions are easily reached, and what misunderstandings arise, if you do not first ask for the reasons for a choice?

Steps to Take

1. Determine whether you are in a position to expand any of your current habits. To plan for this, use the grid from Chapter 3. Set dates to revisit your plan and ensure that you are not allowing things to slip or stagnate.
2. Plan ahead of time your strategies for keystone habits and any new critical thinking habits you are incorporating. Determine where and when you are most likely to give up or feel like you are putting in too much effort. Make a plan and post it somewhere you can see it.
3. Keep in mind that you want those habits to remain as shiny, new, and exciting as they were when you planned and started them. You want to prevent these habits from devaluing and

being taken for granted, just as you would with a new car. Make your maintenance schedule a habit as well.

There are numerous ways to improve our critical thinking skills and turn them into habits that last longer than a season.

Just as good car maintenance can keep an older model looking and running like new, good long-standing habits can keep your mind active and ready to learn whatever new skills and information you require to perform at your best.

Summary of the Chapter
- Be aware that if there is no maintenance plan in place for your tasks, body, and mind, habits can slip over time.
- Remind yourself of your true passion and drive to determine the worth of your habits.
- Your friends and your own mind can either help or hinder you. Control both of these to concentrate on positive influences.
- Tell yourself that this is your new long-term system and give it the attention it deserves. Dropping habits will do you little good in the long run.

5
BUILDING A BETTER BRAIN - PUSH THOSE HABITS HIGHER

"Knowing a great deal is not the same as being smart; intelligence is not information alone but judgement, the manner in which information is collected and used" - Carl Sagan

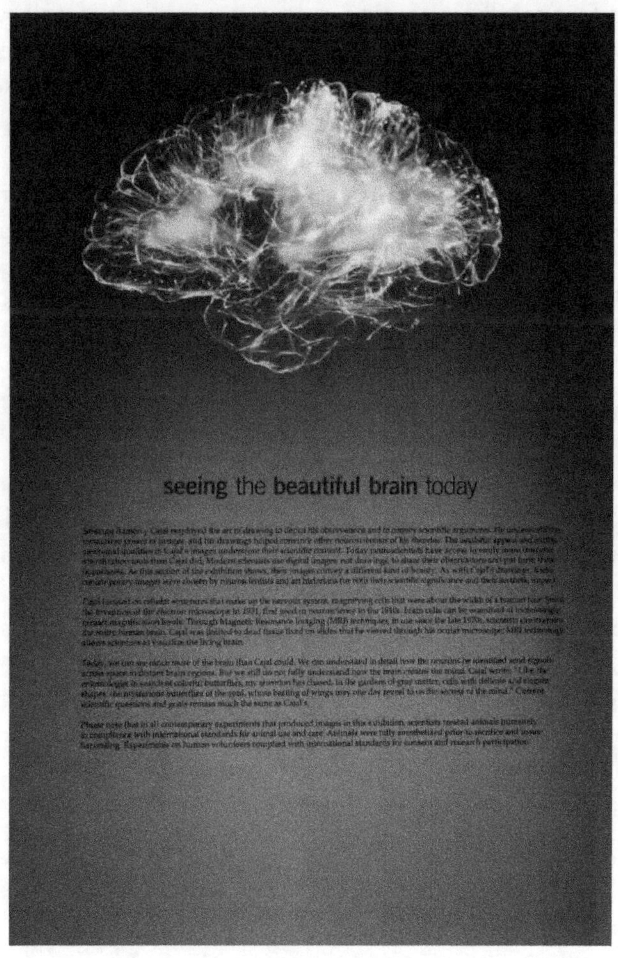

Can you imagine suddenly ceasing to learn? You would be unable to do anything you have not already worked out from this point forward. Nothing, not even asking questions to find answers to unknowns. Life would become extremely difficult very quickly!

We naturally pick up new names for new acquaintances, new routes to new destinations, new lyrics to new songs, and new techniques for new technology. When you accomplish any of these goals, whether it's finding a shortcut that saves you a few minutes on your way home or perfecting a dance move, you'll feel a sense of accomplishment. Humans are hardwired to learn and enjoy doing so.

People frequently use common language against learning, which is surprising given their natural ability to build on and improve previous understanding and skills. They portray learning as a chore, something that only students do, something that is difficult and boring.

Learning is what excites us in life, that sense of new discovery, except when we call it learning! Do you think of learning as a chore or as something to look forward to? Building on your new critical thinking habits will be much easier if you can make learning sound like a treat for your mind.

Critical thinking habits, like a good exercise routine, must be extended in order to continue to challenge you.

To succeed in learning anything, you must persevere and gradually push yourself further. Once you've established the habits with the habit loop and embedded them with trackers or accountability methods, you'll need to extend them so that they challenge you.

The key figure for assessments in 'The Principles of Instruction,' widely regarded as a key summary of good practice in teaching and learning, is an 80 percent success rate. 70% indicates that the assessment is too difficult. 95 percent indicates that it is far too simple. You learn best when the tasks you do present some difficulty, but not so much that you feel like you're failing.

Extending your critical thinking habits entails honing that skill. You should slightly increase the difficulty of that routine so that it reaches your target of 80%. Your goal is to keep it interesting. If you push yourself too hard, you will likely give up and the habit will not become ingrained.

If it's too easy, you won't feel like you're progressing; the habit will lose value and eventually fade away. Remember that good habits are those that are simple to implement and rewarding. Continue to push yourself to gradually improve your limits.

Consider the Greeks

The Socratic method is one that you can incorporate into many aspects of your life. Socrates, the Greek philosopher credited with being a forerunner of modern moral thinking, developed this over 2,500 years ago, and it serves as a framework for successful high-level conversational 'arguments.' These can be internal or external debates with others.

Socratic 'arguments' are not the same as modern-day arguments; this is not about shouting or getting your own way. It is about a cooperative argument in which you ask questions to elicit deeper thought from the person with whom you are conversing. Even if you have different starting points, you are working together to discover the truth.

The mindset you must adopt is similar to that of a coach. You want to ask questions that will help the other person figure out the answers for themselves. You are not there to provide them with answers.
In an ideal world, they will do the same to you.

The method is summarized below:
- Step 1 'wonder' - what is the question for which you are looking for an answer?
- Step 2 'hypothesis' - what do you believe the answer is and why?
- Step 3 is 'cross-examination,' in which questions are asked and evidence is gathered to help determine the validity of the

hypothesis. This is the bulk of your discussion and is also known as 'elenchus,' the Greek word for this type of debate.
- Step 4 is to reach a verdict,' which means determining whether or not the hypothesis can withstand scrutiny.
- Step 5: 'What next?' You may need to take action, ask another question, or propose a new hypothesis.

It is no coincidence that the critical thinking and scientific methods from Chapter 1 are similar. Both of these are based on the Socratic method. You can still use the original method to structure your conversations and your thinking as a framework for excellent debates.

HITT Improve Your Brainpower

Many activities and games can aid in the development of critical thinking skills. Many of them are highly sociable and classify their time as leisure rather than learning time, but they actually use it for both. The best part about wisely choosing your pastimes is that critical thinking skills are then part of your entire life, not just for the development of work or academic pursuits. This is how to make thinking a habit and a thread that runs throughout your life.

Many activities will also allow you to meet people who share your interests, making it easier to have meaningful conversations. You will build a more diverse social network and expose yourself to a wider range of opportunities.

Extend A Habit of Critical Reading

1. Join a book club or find a reading partner with the explicit expectation that you will select more difficult texts and thoroughly review them. Make time for this. Many books have questions available online to facilitate group discussion, and some have them specifically at the end of the book for this purpose. If you want to go deeper into key themes and interpretations, you can use the Socratic method. If having a conversation with a real person is too much for you, you can find podcasts or videos of many book reviews and discussions of both classic and popular books.

2. Enroll in a literature course, either formally or informally if you have the ability and desire to do so. Many universities offer online courses, some of which are free. Oxford University in the United Kingdom, for example, offers a specialized online course for developing critical reading skills.

3. Take part in word games. Examine a news report and determine which word choice is critical to the message being communicated. A good way to do this is to consider which words you could change to give the story a new twist. It's a fun way for you to practice text analysis in short bursts.

Extend a Critical Writing Habit

1. Write online product and service reviews. Aim for a professional response and audience. This will assist you in considering word choice and developing a broader range of descriptive language.

2. Enroll in a writing or editing class, either in person or online. What is important here is that you have assigned tasks as part of your job or professional development. Writing about a topic that has been chosen for you and a specific audience allows you to learn new writing techniques.

3. Try your hand at freelance writing; even if you don't get paid much, it will force you to use a new style and target audience for your journal. Whatever motivates you to continue learning and honing your skills will help you improve.

Extend Your Critical-Thinking Habit

1. Participate in a committee, PTA, local group, or another forum. Accept responsibility for one of the long-term goals and turn it into a system that will lead to that goal as well as long-term success.
   Plan with others how to put the group's or organization's changes to become more system-focused in that area into action.

2. Similarly, you can set out on your own or with friends to identify a local issue that would benefit from a long-term strategy rather

than one-time goals. Plan what you can do and collaborate with others to make it a reality.

3. Contact a local charity or an NGO to find out what their long-term goals are and what you can do to help them put systems in place. It could be organizing a regular fundraiser to provide them with a more consistent income or a regular awareness campaign.

Extend Your Critical-Thinking Habit

1. Go through scientific journals. The scientific method is mirrored in critical thinking. Immersing yourself in the logic of developing discoveries, in particular, if you are not trained as a scientist, is a great way to improve your questioning of what you take for granted. It's a fun way to learn about future possibilities, as much of what's being researched sounds like science fiction.

2. Watch live or archived news night interviews. There are some well-known examples of both the good and the bad!
Identifying what style of questioning elicits key information and what closes down conversations can help you improve your ability to ask good questions.

3. Apply the Socratic method to yourself and others. If possible, practice using the debate style with a friend to improve your ability to cross-examine yourself and others. What you ask isn't as important as how you ask it. You can develop your questioning abilities by listening to podcasts or reading books that discuss the great philosophers' theories. This will allow you to effectively explore and debate a subject.

Extend A Crucial Discussion

1. Listen to a wide range of podcasts. There are an increasing number of sites where you can find these, and the majority of them are free. Many of the most well-known podcasts release new content every day or every week, depending on the subject matter, making it simple to incorporate into a regular routine. TED talks are a great place to start because they cover a wide range of topics that will make you think hard and serve as great conversation starters with others. You can also choose ones to

help you with other skills, such as debates to help you expand your questioning skills, talks to challenge your current opinions, and tutorial style ones to help you with critical reading and writing skills.

2. Look for webinars or in-person seminars on topics of interest to you. There will be talks, which are excellent opportunities to listen, but there will also be opportunities to discuss the ideas of others. This is the time for a discussion.

Extend Critical Thoughts Habit

1. Engage in a conversation with someone you know has an opposing viewpoint but with whom you have a good relationship (to keep things civil). Listen carefully and identify the evidence that they are using to reach a different conclusion than you. Ensure that your goal is to understand the other person's point of view rather than to persuade them to change their mind. Again, the Socratic method can be used as a framework.
2. Go through old schoolbooks or talk to an older relative about what you wanted to do when you were younger. Consider what caused you to change your mind if you took a different route.
3. Watch political debates, either live or on video, or from previous events.

Identify your prior and subsequent opinions; has anything changed, and what evidence caused the change? Investigate the claims made using alternative sources.

Extend A Critical Concluding Habit

1. Examine the decisions of those in positions of authority, whether through the media or autobiographies. This is a great way to figure out how they made decisions and if they had any regrets.
2. Understanding more about other people's decision-making processes allows you to gradually apply the ideas to yourself.

3.   If there are specific thinkers or historical figures whose views you want to emulate, you can decide by asking yourself, "What would X do?" This is not someone you can physically ask, as that is simply passing the buck, but rather a set of ideas or ideals that you can add to your mental checklist to avoid making rash decisions.

No More Mindless Scrolling With Brain Games

Playing a game is sometimes the best way to improve your skills. We all need downtime, and if you can find something you enjoy doing that also improves your mental acuity, it's a win-win situation.

Whether you prefer a physical or digital game, this list should have something for you:

Games from the Past

Chess – whether played with a real board and a real opponent or digitally, chess is a simple game to learn but a difficult one to master. There are numerous apps available that allow you to play against AI or other users.

Go – thought to be the oldest still-played board game, this was first recorded as being played 2,500 years ago. It is simple enough for a child to learn, but mastering it is more difficult than chess.

Again, if you prefer digital to physical gaming, there are online versions available. In a similar way to chess, the game aids in the identification of logical sequences and patterns.

Crossword puzzles- are still popular for a reason. There are plenty of books for a good paper copy, and the New York Times even has an app so you don't have to buy the paper to access the famous crossword puzzle. Try cryptic crossword puzzles for an added mental challenge, where the clues require you to unpick the language and potential double-meanings in the clue before you can begin to consider an answer. If you want to take a different approach, try the app 'Bonza,' which requires you to arrange crossword puzzle fragments.

Sudoku – ranging from simple to difficult, these number puzzles are great for honing logical sequencing skills. You develop working patterns to help you solve the puzzles, and they also improve your attention span. While the puzzles contain numbers, they are not limited to mathematicians; as long as you can count to ten, you can do a Sudoku. There are many puzzle books and apps to choose from; you may want to start with a paper format because it may appear easier to develop your own way of marking the puzzle while working it out.

Apps

Elevate – This app is designed to improve your literacy and numeracy skills in a non-schoollike environment. You can play minigames that are all practical tasks in a gamified setting.

The app adapts your tasks over time to keep you challenged, and there are a variety of areas to work on, including dictation, memory, vocabulary building, estimation, averages, and comprehension. The tasks can be completed quickly, making them easy to incorporate into your existing habit loops and aiding in the formation of a new routine.

Lumosity – Try Lumosity if you want to improve your transferable skills such as prioritising, problem-solving, and memory. The games grade you on your speed, memory, attention, flexibility, and problem-solving abilities. You can easily see a training calendar that can also serve as a habit tracker, and you can play on most platforms thanks to desktop, iOS, and Android versions. The tasks are more game-like than on Elevate, but they frequently train the same skills.

Orixo – For thinking puzzles with relaxing soundtracks, try Orixo if you want to relax while still doing something more brain-building than randomly tapping at a screen. Logisk Studio has created a number of similar games, each with multiple levels to increase the challenge without making you feel stressed.

I Love Hue – This visual puzzle app can help you improve your attention and refocus. It is simple and aesthetically pleasing; it can be used to introduce daily meditation in a non-threatening manner if the thought of staring at nothing is difficult for you. A calm way to gradually hone some important skills.

Peak- is the ultimate high-intensity interval training (HITT) workout for brain training. Short but intense mental workouts to improve focus, memory, problem-solving, mental agility, and more. The games are supported by research conducted by scientists at prestigious UK and US universities.

They have the appearance and feel of games rather than educational tasks with nice graphics, but you are pushed by a coach. As a result, it's some serious brain training.

Happy Neuron- is a program that provides highly personalized feedback; you are assigned a coach who directs you to the most appropriate games for your profile and assists you with motivation and tracking to help you embed the habits. Memory, attention, language, executive functions, visual, spatial, and cross-functional links are the areas of focus. The games are beautifully designed and are available in a variety of languages.

Braingle – If you enjoy brain teasers and riddles, this is the game for you. An online puzzle collection that is constantly being added to and rated by users, this includes a wide variety of puzzles ranging from codes and ciphers to trivia quizzes and strategy games, as well as an online community and a daily email option. Because it is web-based rather than app-based, it is a good choice for the desktop while remaining functional on mobile devices.

Steps to Take

1. Use the grid from Chapter 3 to identify which habits are already in place and which need to be strengthened.
2. Use the suggestions as a guide, but choose only one way to improve one skill. Remember to make it simple and rewarding in

order to activate the Habit Loop!

3. Apply the Socratic method to your inner thoughts first, then to others.

4. Incorporate the necessary steps into your routine, just as you would with a new habit.

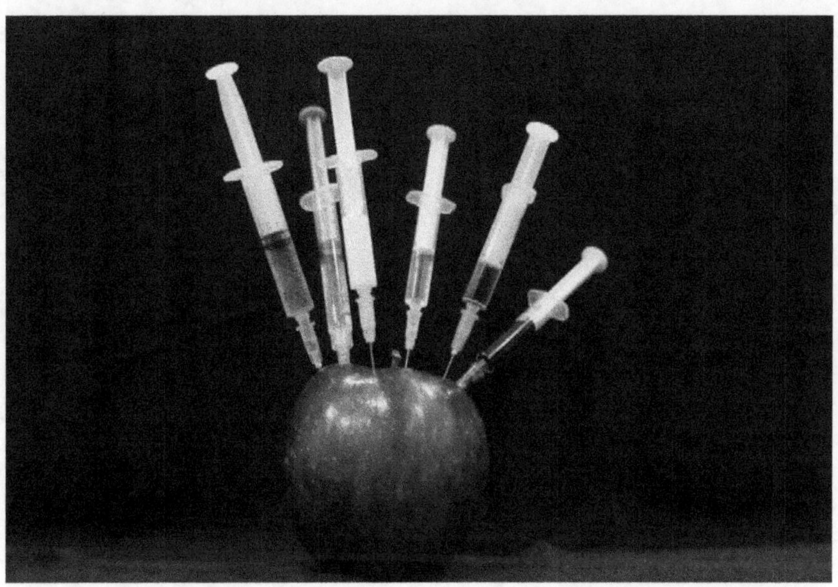

Summary of the Chapter

- To improve your critical thinking skills, aim to extend your critical thinking habits over time. To achieve more, you must continue to challenge yourself, just as you would with a good exercise routine.

- Make certain that you are realistic about the appropriate level of difficulty. If it's too easy, it'll feel unsatisfying and will not elevate you. If you push yourself too hard, you are more likely to give up.

- Plan your action in the same way that you would plan to establish a new habit.

- You can practice critical thinking skills in a variety of enjoyable and social settings. Pick and choose activities that are enjoyable to you.

- Games can help you improve your critical thinking skills. These are especially useful if you want to replace a less productive gaming habit.

CRITICAL THINKING HABIT AIDS: TRACKERS, CALENDARS, APPS AND MORE

"People do not decide their futures, they decide their habits and their habits decide their futures." - F.M. Alexander

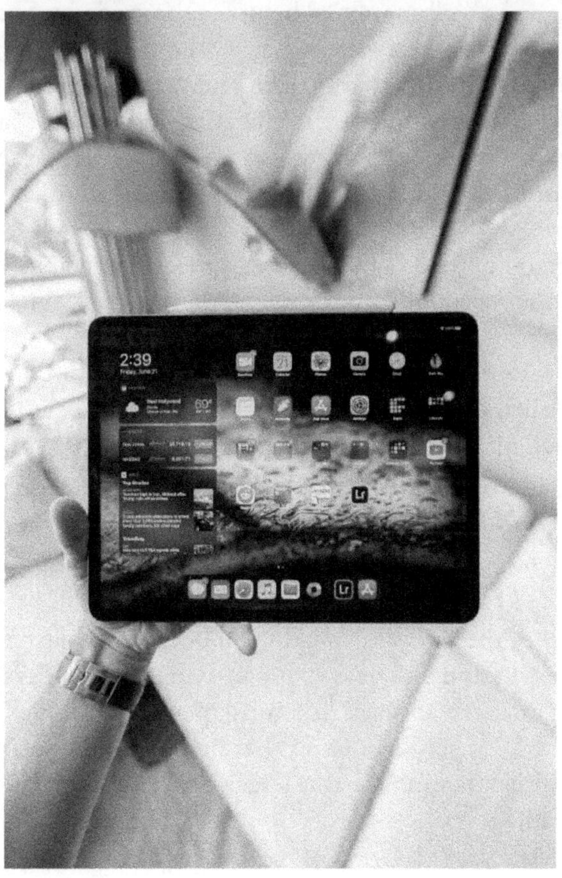

With no wifi and a group of teens on an environmental expedition in the middle of nowhere in Croatia, the conversation quickly turned to how much data they had left on their mobile phones. Nobody wanted to pay any additional fees. Surprisingly, many people were storing data for 'Snapchat streaks.' Unaware of what this was, I inquired as to why it was so significant.

Most had conversations with friends on Snapchat, which meant they had to message every day to keep up their streak.' If they did not message, the counter reset to zero days. That was enough for them to make continued messaging a priority. Despite their remote location and lack of facilities, they did not want to be held responsible for breaking the streak, which could have serious consequences for their friendship.

Snapchat was a well-ingrained habit for the students, and the streaks they could log were crucial to this. Technology companies take advantage of our desire to visualize our 'achievements' in order to entice us to use their products for longer periods of time and see more of their advertisements. However, we can all use the same techniques to embed our own habits, making the process much more enjoyable.

There are numerous paper-based and electronic apps available for planning your days and tracking your progress in breaking or developing a new habit.

So, in a nutshell, why do they work so well? Techniques that are most effective include the following:
- Provide you with a visual cue to remind you to act.
- When you see how far you've come, it's easy to stay motivated.
- Give you satisfaction by documenting your current success.

Using any of these tools can help you because, while new habits can form between 18 and 254 days (with an average of 66 days), they don't become automatic responses for most people until well into the 2-month mark. A lot can happen in that time, so if you can 'mind trick' yourself into maintaining a habit streak by using these tools, you will have an advantage.

Make a plan
Identifying what you need to do and when you need to do it necessitates planning.

This is the starting point for living effectively and efficiently. Using a planner, whether it's a simple calendar, diary, or an app, will help you stay organized. Here are some apps and techniques to consider:

Using a more detailed calendar or planners, such as the 'Hello Day' or 'Unique planners' by Pirongs.

Learn how to bullet journal – a method for planning and tracking almost anything you can think of. There are numerous websites that explain the techniques, as well as books that can walk you through the process of setting it up.

Bullet journals can be purchased with pre-set pages or customized by the user. If you prefer to work on paper and enjoy being both creative and organized, this method is for you.

You can make it into anything you want, and there are social media groups dedicated to sharing successful ideas and tips.

The Habits Scorecard – proposed by author James Clear – allows you to customize your habits record so that you become more aware of your daily behavior. You make a chronological list of your daily routines and then rate each one as effective, ineffective, or neutral. This gives you a better understanding of your various behaviors, which will assist you in becoming the person you want to be. It is useful when planning new habits because it shows where existing habits are so that new ones can be pinned to them, as well as which habits may need to go to make way for better ones.

Monday project management – for professional life planning rather than personal life planning. Good workplace habits necessitate clear communication, well-defined tasks, and task tracking.

This type of software can assist your team in developing systems that streamline workflow.

Ike to-do list app – a simple app that helps you organize your daily and long-term tasks in one location. Because it employs the 'Eisenhower' method, it assists you in categorizing what you need to do in terms of importance and urgency, allowing you to prioritize more easily. If you prefer a paper version, a sample grid is provided below. Make one on a reusable board, or simply jot them down in a diary or planner.

	Urgent	Not Urgent
Important	**Do it now!** These things have an immediate deadline and consequences for not acting immediately. For example: - Dealing with a sick child - Completing an article due in today - Responding to certain calls/emails	**Do it later... plan it in** These things are important and are needed to help you build good systems to achieve your goals. This is where your habit planning comes in. For example: - Reading - Exercise - Meal planning - Personal development activities - Calls to friends and family
Not Important	**Delegate it** These need doing, but not necessarily by you. Outsource if possible! For example: - Grocery shopping/ meal prep - Cleaning - Booking flights/meals out - Certain calls/emails	**Delete it!** These are often the habits you want to drop. They are time-fillers with little real value. Fine in moderation but not good as regular features of your day. For example: - Watching TV - Aimlessly checking social media - Gossip

ClickUp – a cross-platform app for task prioritization, project management, time tracking, and goal setting. You can use it for personal or professional purposes, and you can configure the app accordingly. You can share it with others and integrate it with Outlook, Apple, and Google systems to easily synchronize emails and calendars, reducing work duplication.

Keep track of it

Simply plotting your progress through a Habit Tracker is the best way to follow through on the effectiveness of habit formation or change. Tracking the habit lets you know if you've met your goal of creating, changing, or replacing a habit and alerts you if there are any stumbling blocks along the way. Try a few and, as with any new habit, don't be afraid to switch things up if your first choice doesn't work for you.

Calendars – physical or electronic calendars are the most basic way to track your progress and determine whether you have met your objectives.

You are not even required to write anything.

1. You can mark the completion of a new routine by placing a dot in the corner of the day on a wall calendar or diary. If you have a number to track, different colors or multiple dots can indicate different routines. If you want to make it more obvious, you can cross out days off.

2. To keep a record, you can set up reminders on electronic calendars that you can acknowledge or dismiss. They are less visible than physical ones, but they may be more appropriate if the habit is carried out away from your home or desk, or if you do not want others in your household to know about it.

Journals, like calendars, can be physical paper notebooks or computer files in which you record your habit details and dates. Journals contain more information and are often an extension of calendars. Food journals exercise journals, and reading journals are all common enough that you can buy a ready-made one or simply download and edit a template if you want a customized version.

Journals are especially useful for extending a habit because they allow you to identify areas for improvement much more easily.

Habitica - is a mobile app that helps you track your daily habits and works on the most popular mobile platforms. Their tagline is "gamify your life," and you can earn in-game rewards for sticking to the habits you choose to track. You can use a community to provide support, and you can use this with friends or family to hold you accountable. If you enjoy avatars, mini-games, and digital rewards, this could be a good fit for you. At the time of writing, there were over 4 million users, so there was plenty of help available.

Momentum – a sleek iOS app that focuses on making sure you 'don't break the chain'. You can set reminders, weekly goals, and make notes in the same way that you would in a journal. You can even schedule a week off (if you were sick or on vacation) that will not break your chain, which would have saved the teens in Croatia a lot of trouble! If you like spreadsheets (and who doesn't?), you can export your data for further analysis.

With the ability to synchronize data across multiple devices, this app means business.

Streaks – an award-winning iOS app that allows you to track up to 12 habits. It encourages you to keep 'streaks' of a good habit going to keep you motivated, and it comes with some sleek graphics and synchronization across different Apple devices. Tasks can be scheduled for specific days or on a weekly basis, and a variety of language options are available. It is quick and easy to keep track of what you are doing, and it is simple to identify what you are not doing!

StickK – A 'commitment platform' for iOS and Android that allows you to set goals for yourself and even bet against yourself. There are options for enlisting friends or family members as accountability partners and setting team goals.

Chains is another iOS app that focuses on the 'don't break the chain' method of habit formation. It is simple to use and track, with graphics that can be customized to represent the various habit chains you create.

Steps to Take
1. Consider your previous decisions. Do you need help planning your days, tracking your habits, or playing games to make your brain work a little harder? Choose one area to begin with.

2. Determine whether you prefer pen and paper support, web-based support, or app-based support for your chosen area. Even if you are technologically savvy, you may prefer to keep a physical journal. If you usually write things down, you might prefer a more portable app-based habit tracker. Consider both the practical and emotional aspects. What is most likely to be the most user-friendly?

3. Make a plan for it. When will you make a to-do list if you're going to make one? When are you going to start keeping track of your daily habits? When are you going to play one of the brain games? All of these are still habits that require planning with the Habit Loop. They are habits that aid in the development of other habits.

4. Be willing to try new things. This is only a small sample of what is available for planning, tracking, and playing. Every week, new options are added. Find out what works best for you. Get rid of options that don't work for you. Habits must be simple and rewarding. Habit trackers are no exception!

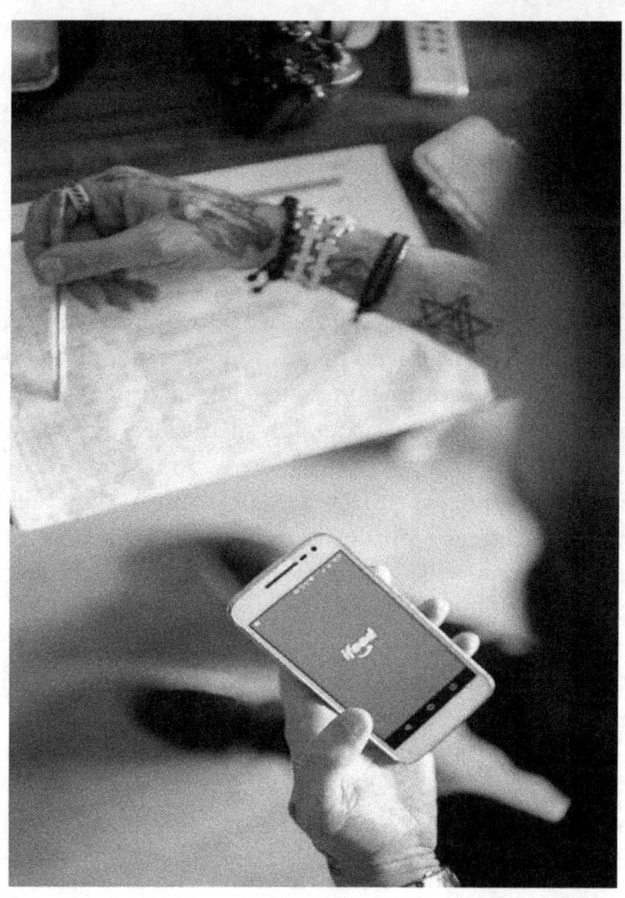

Summary of the Chapter

- Visible rewards provided by habit trackers can improve motivation to complete habits. One of the most effective tools is to try to keep a 'streak' of the desired behavior going.
- Planning ahead of time increases the likelihood of success and improves the ability to prioritize thoughts and actions. Physical and electronic aids can help to make this process faster and more consistent.
- There are both physical and electronic options for tracking habits, planning habits, and playing games to help with cognitive skills.
- All have their applications, and it is up to you to decide which will best support your journey.

AFTERWORD

"Education must enable one to sift and weigh evidence, to discern the true from the false, the real from the unreal and the facts from the fiction. The function of education, therefore, is to teach one to think intensively and to think critically" - Martin Luther King, Jr.

You can now slow down your thinking and break free from automatic decision making and stereotypes. You can improve your critical thinking abilities and characteristics. Building effective habits to help you unwind this way of seeing the world will increase your long-term success, both personally and professionally, without feeling like a chore. You can turn decision-making into a logical process, saving time while improving outcomes and accurately analyzing your own actions.

By incorporating strategies into your daily routines, you will be able to achieve your objectives without them becoming a source of stress. When the right strategies are used, goals are naturally attained. Your relationships can be strengthened by improving your ability to discuss issues rationally and with a more open mind; your horizons can be expanded by actively seeking to understand those who are different from you and removing the barriers erected by societal expectations and preconceptions.

You can effectively manage your time by using planning strategies and tools to make habit maintenance easy and desirable in order to free up your mind and time. No more to-do lists keeping you awake in the middle of the night. You have set aside time to see those you want to see. Deadlines that are easily met. All of this is feasible. A more balanced life can go hand in hand with personal and professional success if you prioritize tasks and use the critical thinking toolkit to build habits that support what you want, eliminate what you don't want, and streamline your days.

So, what are your plans? What does your ideal day or year look like? Even if it appears to be a million miles away from where you are now, it is possible to begin taking the path that leads to your ideal destination. You will be able to reach your ideal destination if you carefully consider your options, take things one step at a time by breaking down your goals into systems, turn these systems into habits, and then track them to ensure that they stick. It takes a shift in mindset from a reactive to an active thinking brain, and then the rest will fall into place.

What comes next? As with any good expedition, you must now decide where you want to go and then figure out what skills you'll need to develop to get there. You can question, plan, gather evidence, analyze your options, and be open to evaluating your chosen path. You understand how to form effective habits and which habits will help you think more clearly. You know how to locate your old auto-pilot and insert a new, upgraded one.

Remember that your life is an experiment. Experiment wisely and thoroughly.